Praise for *Millennium Approaches*

"Daring and dazzling! The most ambitious American play of our time: an epic that ranges from earth to heaven; focuses on politics, sex and religion; transports us to Washington, the Kremlin, the South Bronx, Salt Lake City and Antarctica; deals with Jews, Mormons, WASPs, blacks; switches between realism and fantasy, from the tragedy of AIDS to the camp comedy of drag queens to the death or at least the absconding of God."

—JACK KROLL, *Newsweek*

"Something rare, dangerous and harrowing . . . a roman candle hurled into a drawing room."

—NICHOLAS DE JONGH, *London Evening Standard*

"Fiercely humane, gloriously informed, bitchy, compassionate, uncompromised . . . also falling-down funny."

—LINDA WINER, *Newsday*

"A victory for theatre, for the transforming power of the imagination to turn devastation into beauty."

—JOHN LAHR, *New Yorker*

"An epic theatrical fever dream . . . a cliffhanger that leaves you wanting more."

Praise for *Perestroika*

"*Perestroika* is not only a stunning resolution of the rending human drama of *Millennium Approaches*, but also a true millennial work of art, uplifting, hugely comic and pantheistically religious in a very American style."

—FRANK RICH, *New York Times*

"Playful and profound, extravagantly theatrical and deeply spiritual, witty and compassionate, furious and incredibly smart . . . It's impossible to imagine anyone captivated by the beginning not wanting—*needing*—to go back for the end."

—LINDA WINER, *Newsday*

"*Perestroika* is a masterpiece. Not since Tennessee Williams has a playwright announced his poetic vision with such authority on the Broadway stage."

—JOHN LAHR, *New Yorker*

"A monumental achievement, the work of a defiantly theatrical imagination that has no parallel on television or in the movies. It ennobles Broadway as no other work in recent memory has."

—JEREMY GERARD, *Variety*

"An enormously impressive work of the imagination and intellect, a towering example of what theatre stretched to its full potential can achieve."

—CLIFFORD A. RIDLEY, *Philadelphia Inquirer*

ANGELS in AMERICA

A Gay Fantasia on National Themes

Part One: MILLENNIUM APPROACHES

Part Two: PERESTROIKA

Tony Kushner

Theatre Communications Group

This publication is made possible in part with public funds from
the New York State Council on the Arts, a State Agency.

TCG books are exclusively distributed to the book trade by Consortium
Book Sales and Distribution, 1045 Westgate Dr., St. Paul, MN 55114.

CIP data information is on file at the Library of Congress, Washington, D.C.

Book design by Lisa Govan; compostion by The Sarabande Press

First Combined Paperback Edition, September 2003
Sixth Printing, January 2007

Contents

ANGELS in AMERICA

Part One: MILLENNIUM APPROACHES

The actors, directors and designers who have worked on the play transformed it. What follows is a list of the play's professional productions to date.

Millennium Approaches was first performed in a workshop production presented by Center Theatre Group/Mark Taper Forum, May 1990. It was directed by Oskar Eustis. Sets were designed by Mark Wendlend, costumes by Lydia Tanji, lights by Casey Cowan and Brian Gale, and music by Nathan Birnbaum. The cast was as follows:

ROY COHN	*Richard Frank*
JOE PITT	*Jeffrey King*
HARPER PITT	*Lorri Holt*
BELIZE	*Harry Waters Jr.*
LOUIS IRONSON	*Jon Matthews*
PRIOR WALTER	*Stephen Spinella*
HANNAH PITT	*Kathleen Chalfant*
THE ANGEL	*Ellen McLaughlin*

The World Premiere of *Millennium Approaches* was presented by The Eureka Theatre Company, May 1991. It was directed by David Esbjornson. Sets were designed by Tom Kamm, costumes by Sandra Woodall, and lights by Jack Carpenter and Jim Cave. The cast was as follows:

ROY COHN	*John Bellucci*
JOE PITT	*Michael Scott Ryan*
HARPER PITT	*Anne Darragh*
BELIZE	*Harry Waters Jr.*
LOUIS IRONSON	*Michael Ornstein*
PRIOR WALTER	*Stephen Spinella*
HANNAH PITT	*Kathleen Chalfant*
THE ANGEL	*Ellen McLaughlin*

The play opened in London, January 1992, in a production at the Royal National Theatre of Great Britain, directed by Declan Donellan, designed by Nick Ormerod, with music by Paddy Cuneen and lights by Mick Hughes. The cast was as follows:

ROY COHN	*Henry Goodman*
JOE PITT	*Nick Reding*
HARPER PITT	*Felicity Montague*
BELIZE	*Joe Mydell*
LOUIS	*Marcus D'Amico*
PRIOR WALTER	*Sean Chapman*
HANNAH PITT	*Rosemary Martin*
THE ANGEL	*Nancy Crane*
THE RABBI, HENRY, MARTIN HELLER, PRIOR I	*Jeffrey Chiswick*

The first production of *Angels in America*, Parts One and Two, was presented at the Mark Taper Forum in Los Angeles, directed by Oskar Eustis and Tony Taccone. The sets were designed by John Conklin, lights by Pat Collins, costumes by Gabriel Berry, and music by Mel Marvin. The cast was as follows:

ROY COHN	*Ron Leibman*
JOE PITT	*Jeffrey King*
HARPER PITT	*Cynthia Mace*
BELIZE	*K. Todd Freeman*
LOUIS IRONSON	*Joe Mantello*
PRIOR WALTER	*Stephen Spinella*
HANNAH PITT	*Kathleen Chalfant*
THE ANGEL	*Ellen McLaughlin*

Millennium Approaches opened in New York at the Walter Kerr Theatre in April 1993, in a production directed by George C. Wolfe. The sets were by Robin Wagner, the lights by Jules Fisher and costumes by Toni-Leslie James. The cast was as follows:

ROY COHN	*Ron Leibman*
JOE PITT	*David Marshall Grant*
HARPER PITT	*Marcia Gay Harden*
BELIZE	*Jeffrey Wright*
LOUIS IRONSON	*Joe Mantello*
PRIOR WALTER	*Stephen Spinella*
HANNAH PITT	*Kathleen Chalfant*
THE ANGEL	*Ellen McLaughlin*

The national touring production of *Millennium Approaches* began its run on September 25, 1994, at the Royal George Theatre in Chicago. It was directed by Michael Mayer, with sets by David Gallo, lights by Brian MacDevitt, costumes by Michael Krass and music by Michael Ward. The cast was as follows:

ROY COHN	*Jonathan Hadary*
JOE PITT	*Philip Earl Johnson*
HARPER PITT	*Kate Goehring*
BELIZE	*Reg Flowers*
LOUIS IRONSON	*Peter Birkenhead*
PRIOR WALTER	*Robert Sella*
HANNAH PITT	*Barbara Robertson*
THE ANGEL	*Carolyn Swift*

ACKNOWLEDGMENTS

I've been working on *Angels in America*, of which *Millennium Approaches* is the first part, for several years, and in the process have accumulated many debts:

I received generous support during the writing of this play in the form of grants from the National Endowment for the Arts, the Gerbode Foundation, and the Fund for New American Plays/American Express. Further financial and abundant emotional support came from my parents, Bill and Sylvia Kushner, Martha Deutscher, and Dot and Jerry Edelstien. Joyce Ketay the Wonder-Agent, and her associate Carl Mulert have been awesomely protective and farsighted; and from Jim Nicola of New York Theatre Workshop I have gotten wonderfully smart advice.

Gordon Davidson and the staff of the Mark Taper Forum provided the play and its author with the best circumstances for development and production any artist could hope for.

Richard Eyre and the staff of the National Theatre made a timorous and occasionally querulous visitor to British theatre feel at home. Declan Donellan and Nick Ormerod made the play dance.

Angels has benefited from the dramaturgical work of Roberta Levitow, Philip Kan Gotanda, Leon Katz and Ellen McLaughlin; and K. C. Davis contributed dramaturgy, dedication and Radical Queerness.

Sigrid Wurschmidt, actress extraordinaire and angel of light, remains with the play though she's left the world.

Bill Anderson, Andy Holland, Ian Kramer, Peter Minthorn, Sam Sommer and John Ryan are everywhere in this play.

David Esbjornson helped shape the final version of *Millennium* and brought it, fabulously, to San Francisco.

Tony Taccone brought craft, clarity and *menschlichkeit* to Los Angeles.

Oskar Eustis's guidance, talents, intelligence and friendship have been indispensable; he called *Angels in America* into being, shepherded it through many perilous places, and brought it safely home. Without him it would have neither been begun nor completed.

To Kimberly T. Flynn, for intellectual and political instruction, and for the difficult education of my heart, I owe my profoundest debts of gratitude.

Millennium Approaches is for Mark Bronnenberg, my former lover, my forever friend, my safe haven and my favorite homosexual.

THE CHARACTERS

ROY M. COHN, *a successful New York lawyer and unofficial power broker.*

JOSEPH PORTER PITT, *chief clerk for Justice Theodore Wilson of the Federal Court of Appeals, Second Circuit.*

HARPER AMATY PITT, *Joe's wife, an agoraphobic with a mild Valium addiction.*

LOUIS IRONSON, *a word processor working for the Second Circuit Court of Appeals.*

PRIOR WALTER, *Louis's boyfriend. Occasionally works as a club designer or caterer, otherwise lives very modestly but with great style off a small trust fund.*

HANNAH PORTER PITT, *Joe's mother, currently residing in Salt Lake City, living off her deceased husband's army pension.*

BELIZE, *a former drag queen and former lover of Prior's. A registered nurse. Belize's name was originally Norman Arriaga; Belize is a drag name that stuck.*

THE ANGEL, *four divine emanations, Fluor, Phosphor, Lumen and Candle; manifest in One: the Continental Principality of America. She has magnificent steel-gray wings.*

Other Characters in Part One

RABBI ISIDOR CHEMELWITZ, *an orthodox Jewish rabbi, played by the actor playing Hannah.*

MR. LIES, *Harper's imaginary friend, a travel agent, who in style of dress and speech suggests a jazz musician; he always wears a large lapel badge emblazoned "IOTA" (The International Order of Travel Agents). He is played by the actor playing Belize.*

THE MAN IN THE PARK, *played by the actor playing Prior.*

THE VOICE, *the voice of The Angel.*

HENRY, *Roy's doctor, played by the actor playing Hannah.*

EMILY, *a nurse, played by the actor playing The Angel.*

MARTIN HELLER, *a Reagan Administration Justice Department flackman, played by the actor playing Harper.*

SISTER ELLA CHAPTER, *a Salt Lake City real-estate saleswoman, played by the actor playing The Angel.*

PRIOR 1, *the ghost of a dead Prior Walter from the 13th century, played by the actor playing Joe. He is a blunt, gloomy medieval farmer with a guttural Yorkshire accent.*

PRIOR 2, *the ghost of a dead Prior Walter from the 17th century, played by the actor playing Roy. He is a Londoner, sophisticated, with a High British accent.*

THE ESKIMO, *played by the actor playing Joe.*

THE WOMAN IN THE SOUTH BRONX, *played by the actor playing The Angel.*

ETHEL ROSENBERG, *played by the actor playing Hannah.*

Playwright's notes

A DISCLAIMER: Roy M. Cohn, the character, is based on the late Roy M. Cohn (1927-1986), who was all too real; for the most part the acts attributed to the character Roy, such as his illegal conferences with Judge Kaufmann during the trial of Ethel Rosenberg, are to be found in the historical record. But this Roy is a work of dramatic fiction; his words are my invention, and liberties have been taken.

A NOTE ABOUT THE STAGING: The play benefits from a pared-down style of presentation, with minimal scenery and scene shifts done rapidly (no blackouts!), employing the cast as well as stagehands—which makes for an actor-driven event, as this must be. The moments of magic—the appearance and disappearance of Mr. Lies and the ghosts, the Book hallucination, and the ending—are to be fully realized, as bits of wonderful *theatrical* illusion—which means it's OK if the wires show, and maybe it's good that they do, but the magic should at the same time be thoroughly amazing.

In a murderous time
    the heart breaks and breaks
    and lives by breaking.
       —Stanley Kunitz
       "The Testing-Tree"

ACT ONE:

Bad News

October–November 1985

Scene 1

The last days of October. Rabbi Isidor Chemelwitz alone onstage with a small coffin. It is a rough pine box with two wooden pegs, one at the foot and one at the head, holding the lid in place. A prayer shawl embroidered with a Star of David is draped over the lid, and by the head a yarzheit candle is burning.

RABBI ISIDOR CHEMELWITZ *(He speaks sonorously, with a heavy Eastern European accent, unapologetically consulting a sheet of notes for the family names)*: Hello and good morning. I am Rabbi Isidor Chemelwitz of the Bronx Home for Aged Hebrews. We are here this morning to pay respects at the passing of Sarah Ironson, devoted wife of Benjamin Ironson, also deceased, loving and caring mother of her sons Morris, Abraham, and Samuel, and her daughters Esther and Rachel; beloved grandmother of Max, Mark, Louis, Lisa, Maria . . . uh . . . Lesley, Angela, Doris,

15

Luke and Eric. *(Looks more closely at paper)* Eric? This is a Jewish name? *(Shrugs)* Eric. A large and loving family. We assemble that we may mourn collectively this good and righteous woman.

(He looks at the coffin)

This woman. I did not know this woman. I cannot accurately describe her attributes, nor do justice to her dimensions. She was. . . . Well, in the Bronx Home of Aged Hebrews are many like this, the old, and to many I speak but not to be frank with this one. She preferred silence. So I do not know her and yet I know her. She was . . .

(He touches the coffin)

. . . not a person but a whole kind of person, the ones who crossed the ocean, who brought with us to America the villages of Russia and Lithuania—and how we struggled, and how we fought, for the family, for the Jewish home, so that you would not grow up *here*, in this strange place, in the melting pot where nothing melted. Descendants of this immigrant woman, you do not grow up in America, you and your children and their children with the goyische names. You do not live in America. No such place exists. Your clay is the clay of some Litvak shtetl, your air the air of the steppes—because she carried the old world on her back across the ocean, in a boat, and she put it down on Grand Concourse Avenue, or in Flatbush, and she worked that earth into your bones, and you pass it to your children, this ancient, ancient culture and home.

(Little pause)

You can never make that crossing that she made, for such Great Voyages in this world do not any more exist. But every day of your lives the miles that voyage between that place and this one you cross. Every day. You understand me? In you that journey is.

So . . .

She was the last of the Mohicans, this one was. Pretty soon . . . all the old will be dead.

Scene 2

Same day. Roy and Joe in Roy's office. Roy at an impressive desk, bare except for a very elaborate phone system, rows and rows of flashing buttons which bleep and beep and whistle incessantly, making chaotic music underneath Roy's conversations. Joe is sitting, waiting. Roy conducts business with great energy, impatience and sensual abandon: gesticulating, shouting, cajoling, crooning, playing the phone, receiver and hold button with virtuosity and love.

ROY *(Hitting a button)*: Hold. *(To Joe)* I wish I was an octopus, a fucking octopus. Eight loving arms and all those suckers. Know what I mean?

JOE: No, I . . .

ROY *(Gesturing to a deli platter of little sandwiches on his desk)*: You want lunch?

JOE: No, that's OK really I just . . .

ROY *(Hitting a button)*: Ailene? Roy Cohn. Now what kind of a greeting is. . . . I thought we were friends, Ai. . . . Look Mrs. Soffer you don't have to get. . . . You're upset. You're yelling. You'll aggravate your condition, you shouldn't yell, you'll pop little blood vessels in your face if you yell. . . . No that was a joke, Mrs. Soffer, I was joking. . . . I already apologized sixteen times for that, Mrs. Soffer, you . . . *(While she's fulminating, Roy covers the mouthpiece with his hand and talks to Joe)* This'll take a minute, *eat* already, what is this tasty sandwich here it's— *(He takes a bite of a sandwich)* Mmmmm, liver or some. . . . Here.

(He pitches the sandwich to Joe, who catches it and returns it to the platter.)

ROY *(Back to Mrs. Soffer)*: Uh huh, uh huh. . . . No, I already told you, it wasn't a vacation, it was business, Mrs. Soffer, I have clients in Haiti, Mrs. Soffer, I. . . . Listen, Ailene, YOU THINK I'M THE ONLY GODDAM LAWYER IN HISTORY EVER MISSED A COURT DATE? Don't make such a big fucking. . . . Hold. *(He hits the hold button)* You HAG!

JOE: If this is a bad time . . .

ROY: *Bad* time? This is a *good* time! *(Button)* Baby doll, get me. . . . Oh fuck, wait . . . *(Button, button)* Hello? Yah. Sorry to keep you holding, Judge Hollins, I. . . . Oh *Mrs.* Hollins, sorry dear deep voice you got. Enjoying your visit? *(Hand over mouthpiece again, to Joe)* She sounds like a truckdriver and he sounds like Kate Smith, very confusing. Nixon appointed him, all the geeks are Nixon appointees . . . *(To Mrs. Hollins)* Yeah yeah right good so how many tickets dear? Seven. For what, *Cats, 42nd Street*, what? No you wouldn't like *La Cage*, trust me, I know. Oh for godsake. . . . Hold. *(Button, button)* Baby doll, seven for *Cats* or something, anything hard to get, I don't give a fuck what and neither will they. *(Button; to Joe)* You see *La Cage*?

JOE: No, I . . .

ROY: Fabulous. Best thing on Broadway. Maybe ever. *(Button)* Who? Aw, Jesus H. Christ, Harry, *no*, Harry, Judge John Francis Grimes, Manhattan Family Court. Do I have to do every goddam thing myself? *Touch* the bastard, Harry, and don't call me on this line again, I told you not to . . .

JOE *(Starting to get up)*: Roy, uh, should I wait outside or . . .

ROY *(To Joe)*: Oh sit. *(To Harry)* You hold. I pay you to hold fuck you Harry you jerk. *(Button)* Half-wit dick-brain. *(Instantly philosophical)* I see the universe, Joe, as a kind of sandstorm in outer space with winds of mega-hurricane velocity, but instead of grains of sand it's shards and splinters of glass. You ever feel that way? Ever have one of those days?

JOE: I'm not sure I . . .

ROY: So how's life in Appeals? How's the Judge?

JOE: He sends his best.

ROY: He's a good man. Loyal. Not the brightest man on the bench, but he has manners. And a nice head of silver hair.

JOE: He gives me a lot of responsibility.

ROY: Yeah, like writing his decisions and signing his name.

JOE: Well . . .

ROY: He's a nice guy. And you cover admirably.

JOE: Well, thanks, Roy, I . . .

ROY *(Button)*: Yah? Who is *this*? Well who the fuck are *you*? Hold— *(Button)* Harry? Eighty-seven grand, something like that. Fuck him. Eat me. New Jersey, chain of porno film stores in, uh, Weehawken. That's—Harry, that's the beauty of the law. *(Button)* So, baby doll, what? *Cats?* Bleah. *(Button) Cats!* It's about cats. Singing cats, you'll love it. Eight o'clock, the theatre's always at eight. *(Button)* Fucking tourists. *(Button, then to Joe)* Oh live a little, Joe, *eat* something for Christ sake—

JOE: Um, Roy, could you . . .

ROY: What? *(To Harry)* Hold a minute. *(Button)* Mrs. Soffer? Mrs. . . . *(Button)* God-fucking-dammit to hell, where is . . .

JOE *(Overlapping)*: Roy, I'd really appreciate it if . . .

ROY *(Overlapping)*: Well she was here a minute ago, baby doll, see if . . .

(The phone starts making three different beeping sounds, all at once.)

ROY *(Smashing buttons)*: Jesus fuck this goddam thing . . .

JOE *(Overlapping)*: I really wish you wouldn't . . .

ROY *(Overlapping)*: Baby doll? Ring the *Post* get me Suzy see if . . .

(The phone starts whistling loudly.)

ROY: CHRIST!

JOE: *Roy.*

ROY *(Into receiver)*: Hold. *(Button; to Joe)* What?

JOE: Could you please not take the Lord's name in vain?

(Pause)

I'm sorry. But please. At least while I'm . . .

ROY *(Laughs, then)*: Right. Sorry. Fuck.

Only in America. *(Punches a button)* Baby doll, tell 'em all to fuck off. Tell 'em I died. You handle Mrs. Soffer. Tell her it's on the way. Tell her I'm schtupping the judge. I'll call her back. I *will* call her. I *know* how much I borrowed. She's got four hundred times that stuffed up her. . . . Yeah, tell her I said that. *(Button. The phone is silent)*

So, Joe.

JOE: I'm sorry Roy, I just . . .

ROY: No no no no, principles count, I respect principles, I'm not religious but I like God and God likes me. Baptist, Catholic?

JOE: Mormon.

ROY: Mormon. Delectable. Absolutely. Only in America. So, Joe. Whattya think?

JOE: It's . . . well . . .

ROY: Crazy life.

JOE: Chaotic.

ROY: Well but God bless chaos. Right?

JOE: Ummm . . .

ROY: Huh. Mormons. I knew Mormons, in, um, Nevada.

JOE: Utah, mostly.

ROY: No, these Mormons were in Vegas.

So. So, how'd you like to go to Washington and work for the Justice Department?

JOE: Sorry?

ROY: How'd you like to go to Washington and work for the Justice Department? All I gotta do is pick up the phone, talk to Ed, and you're in.

JOE: In . . . what, exactly?

ROY: Associate Assistant Something Big. Internal Affairs, heart of the woods, something nice with clout.

JOE: Ed . . . ?

ROY: Meese. The Attorney General.

JOE: Oh.

ROY: I just have to pick up the phone . . .

JOE: I have to think.

ROY: Of course.

(Pause)

It's a great time to be in Washington, Joe.

JOE: Roy, it's incredibly exciting . . .

ROY: And it would mean something to me. You understand?

(Little pause.)

JOE: I . . . can't say how much I appreciate this Roy, I'm sort of . . . well, stunned, I mean. . . . Thanks, Roy. But I have to give it some thought. I have to ask my wife.

ROY: Your wife. Of course.

JOE: But I really appreciate . . .

ROY: Of course. Talk to your wife.

Scene 3

Later that day. Harper at home, alone. She is listening to the radio and talking to herself, as she often does. She speaks to the audience.

HARPER: People who are lonely, people left alone, sit talking nonsense to the air, imagining . . . beautiful systems dying, old fixed orders spiraling apart . . .

When you look at the ozone layer, from outside, from a spaceship, it looks like a pale blue halo, a gentle, shimmering aureole encircling the atmosphere encircling the earth. Thirty miles above our heads, a thin layer of three-atom oxygen molecules, product of photosynthesis, which explains the fussy vegetable preference for visible light, its rejection of darker rays and emanations. Danger from without. It's a kind of gift, from God, the crowning touch to the creation of the world: guardian angels, hands linked, make a spherical net, a blue-green nesting orb, a shell of safety for life itself. But everywhere, things are collapsing, lies surfacing, systems of defense giving way. . . . This is why, Joe, this is why I shouldn't be left alone.

(Little pause)

I'd like to go traveling. Leave you behind to worry. I'll send postcards with strange stamps and tantalizing messages on the back. "Later maybe." "Nevermore . . ."

(Mr. Lies, a travel agent, appears.)

HARPER: Oh! You startled me!

MR. LIES: Cash, check or credit card?

HARPER: I remember you. You're from Salt Lake. You sold us the plane tickets when we flew here. What are you doing in Brooklyn?

MR. LIES: You said you wanted to travel . . .

HARPER: And here you are. How thoughtful.

MR. LIES: Mr. Lies. Of the International Order of Travel Agents. We mobilize the globe, we set people adrift, we stir the populace and send nomads eddying across the planet. We are adepts of motion, acolytes of the flux. Cash, check or credit card. Name your destination.

HARPER: Antarctica, maybe. I want to see the hole in the ozone. I heard on the radio . . .

MR. LIES *(He has a computer terminal in his briefcase)*: I can arrange a guided tour. Now?

HARPER: Soon. Maybe soon. I'm not safe here you see. Things aren't right with me. Weird stuff happens . . .

MR. LIES: Like?

HARPER: Well, like you, for instance. Just appearing. Or last week . . . well never mind.

People are like planets, you need a thick skin. Things

get to me, Joe stays away and now. . . . Well look. My
dreams are talking back to me.

MR. LIES: It's the price of rootlessness. Motion sickness. The
only cure: to keep moving.

HARPER: I'm undecided. I feel . . . that something's going
to give. It's 1985. Fifteen years till the third millennium. Maybe Christ will come again. Maybe seeds will be
planted, maybe there'll be harvests then, maybe early figs
to eat, maybe new life, maybe fresh blood, maybe companionship and love and protection, safety from what's
outside, maybe the door will hold, or maybe . . . maybe
the troubles will come, and the end will come, and the sky
will collapse and there will be terrible rains and showers of
poison light, or maybe my life is really fine, maybe Joe
loves me and I'm only crazy thinking otherwise, or maybe
not, maybe it's even worse than I know, maybe . . . I want
to know, maybe I don't. The suspense, Mr. Lies, it's
killing me.

MR. LIES: I suggest a vacation.

HARPER *(Hearing something)*: That was the elevator. Oh God, I
should fix myself up, I. . . . You have to go, you shouldn't
be here . . . you aren't even real.

MR. LIES: Call me when you decide . . .

HARPER: Go!

(The Travel Agent vanishes as Joe enters.)

JOE: Buddy?
Buddy? Sorry I'm late. I was just . . . out. Walking.
Are you mad?

HARPER: I got a little anxious.

JOE: Buddy kiss.

(They kiss.)

JOE: Nothing to get anxious about.

So. So how'd you like to move to Washington?

Scene 4

Same day. Louis and Prior outside the funeral home, sitting on a bench, both dressed in funereal finery, talking. The funeral service for Sarah Ironson has just concluded and Louis is about to leave for the cemetery.

LOUIS: My grandmother actually saw Emma Goldman speak. In Yiddish. But all Grandma could remember was that she spoke well and wore a hat.

What a weird service. That rabbi . . .

PRIOR: A definite find. Get his number when you go to the graveyard. I want him to bury me.

LOUIS: Better head out there. Everyone gets to put dirt on the coffin once it's lowered in.

PRIOR: Oooh. Cemetery fun. Don't want to miss that.

LOUIS: It's an old Jewish custom to express love. Here, Grandma, have a shovelful. Latecomers run the risk of finding the grave completely filled.

She was pretty crazy. She was up there in that home for ten years, talking to herself. I never visited. She looked too much like my mother.

PRIOR *(Hugs him)*: Poor Louis. I'm sorry your grandma is dead.

LOUIS: Tiny little coffin, huh?

Sorry I didn't introduce you to. . . . I always get so closety at these family things.

PRIOR: Butch. You get butch. *(Imitating)* "Hi Cousin Doris, you don't remember me I'm Lou, Rachel's boy." Lou, not Louis, because if you say Louis they'll hear the sibilant S.

LOUIS: I don't have a . . .

PRIOR: I don't blame you, hiding. Bloodlines. Jewish curses are the worst. I personally would dissolve if anyone ever looked me in the eye and said "Feh." Fortunately WASPs don't say "Feh." Oh and by the way, darling, cousin Doris is a dyke.

LOUIS: No.

Really?

PRIOR: You don't notice anything. If I hadn't spent the last four years fellating you I'd swear you were straight.

LOUIS: You're in a pissy mood. Cat still missing?

(Little pause.)

PRIOR: Not a furball in sight. It's your fault.

LOUIS: It is?

PRIOR: I warned you, Louis. Names are important. Call an animal "Little Sheba" and you can't expect it to stick around. Besides, it's a dog's name.

LOUIS: I wanted a dog in the first place, not a cat. He sprayed my books.

PRIOR: He was a female cat.

LOUIS: Cats are stupid, high-strung predators. Babylonians sealed them up in bricks. Dogs have brains.

PRIOR: Cats have intuition.

LOUIS: A sharp dog is as smart as a really dull two-year-old child.

PRIOR: Cats know when something's wrong.

LOUIS: Only if you stop feeding them.

PRIOR: They know. That's why Sheba left, because she knew.

LOUIS: Knew what?

(Pause.)

PRIOR: I did my best Shirley Booth this morning, floppy slippers, housecoat, curlers, can of Little Friskies; "Come back, Little Sheba, come back. . . ." To no avail. Le chat, elle ne reviendra jamais, jamais . . .
(He removes his jacket, rolls up his sleeve, shows Louis a dark-purple spot on the underside of his arm near the shoulder)
See.

LOUIS: That's just a burst blood vessel.

PRIOR: Not according to the best medical authorities.

LOUIS: What?
(Pause)
Tell me.

PRIOR: K.S., baby. Lesion number one. Lookit. The wine-dark kiss of the angel of death.

LOUIS *(Very softly, holding Prior's arm)*: Oh please . . .

PRIOR: I'm a lesionnaire. The Foreign Lesion. The American Lesion. Lesionnaire's disease.

LOUIS: Stop.

PRIOR: My troubles are lesion.

LOUIS: Will you *stop.*

PRIOR: Don't you think I'm handling this well?
I'm going to die.

LOUIS: Bullshit.

PRIOR: Let go of my arm.

LOUIS: No.

PRIOR: Let go.

LOUIS *(Grabbing Prior, embracing him ferociously)*: No.

PRIOR: I can't find a way to spare you baby. No wall like the wall of hard scientific fact. K.S. Wham. Bang your head on that.

LOUIS: Fuck you. *(Letting go)* Fuck you fuck you fuck you.

PRIOR: Now that's what I like to hear. A mature reaction.
　　　Let's go see if the cat's come home.
　　　Louis?

LOUIS: When did you find this?

PRIOR: I couldn't tell you.

LOUIS: Why?

PRIOR: I was scared, Lou.

LOUIS: Of what?

PRIOR: That you'll leave me.

LOUIS: Oh.

(Little pause.)

PRIOR: Bad timing, funeral and all, but I figured as long as we're on the subject of death . . .

LOUIS: I have to go bury my grandma.

PRIOR: Lou?
　　　(Pause)
　　　Then you'll come home?

LOUIS: Then I'll come home.

Scene 5

Same day, later on. Split scene: Joe and Harper at home; Louis at the cemetery with Rabbi Isidor Chemelwitz and the little coffin.

HARPER: Washington?

JOE: It's an incredible honor, buddy, and . . .

HARPER: I have to think.

JOE: Of course.

HARPER: Say no.

JOE: You said you were going to think about it.

HARPER: I don't want to move to Washington.

JOE: Well I do.

HARPER: It's a giant cemetery, huge white graves and mauso-leums everywhere.

JOE: We could live in Maryland. Or Georgetown.

HARPER: We're happy here.

JOE: That's not really true, buddy, we . . .

HARPER: Well happy enough! Pretend-happy. That's better than nothing.

JOE: It's time to make some changes, Harper.

HARPER: No changes. Why?

JOE: I've been chief clerk for four years. I make twenty-nine thousand dollars a year. That's ridiculous. I graduated fourth in my class and I make less than anyone I know. And I'm . . . I'm tired of being a clerk, I want to go where something good is happening.

HARPER: Nothing good happens in Washington. We'll forget church teachings and buy furniture at . . . at *Conran's* and become yuppies. I have too much to do here.

JOE: Like what?

HARPER: I *do* have things . . .

JOE: What things?

HARPER: I have to finish painting the bedroom.

JOE: You've been painting in there for over a year.

HARPER: I know, I. . . . It just isn't done because I never get time to finish it.

JOE: Oh that's . . . that doesn't make sense. You have all the time in the world. You could finish it when I'm at work.

HARPER: I'm afraid to go in there alone.

JOE: Afraid of what?

HARPER: I heard someone in there. Metal scraping on the wall. A man with a knife, maybe.

JOE: There's no one in the bedroom, Harper.

HARPER: Not now.

JOE: Not this morning either.

HARPER: How do you know? You were at work this morning. There's something creepy about this place. Remember *Rosemary's Baby*?

JOE: *Rosemary's Baby*?

HARPER: Our apartment looks like that one. Wasn't that apartment in Brooklyn?

JOE: No, it was . . .

HARPER: Well, it looked like this. It did.

JOE: Then let's move.

HARPER: Georgetown's worse. *The Exorcist* was in Georgetown.

JOE: The devil, everywhere you turn, huh, buddy.

HARPER: Yeah. Everywhere.

JOE: How many pills today, buddy?

HARPER: None. One. Three. Only three.

LOUIS (*Pointing at the coffin*): Why are there just two little wooden pegs holding the lid down?

RABBI ISIDOR CHEMELWITZ: So she can get out easier if she wants to.

LOUIS: I hope she stays put.

  I pretended for years that she was already dead. When they called to say she had died it was a surprise. I abandoned her.

RABBI ISIDOR CHEMELWITZ: "Sharfer vi di tson fun a shlang iz an umdankbar kind!"

LOUIS: I don't speak Yiddish.

RABBI ISIDOR CHEMELWITZ: Sharper than the serpent's tooth is the ingratitude of children. Shakespeare. *Kenig Lear*.

LOUIS: Rabbi, what does the Holy Writ say about someone who abandons someone he loves at a time of great need?

RABBI ISIDOR CHEMELWITZ: Why would a person do such a thing?

LOUIS: Because he has to.

Maybe because this person's sense of the world, that it will change for the better with struggle, maybe a person who has this neo-Hegelian positivist sense of constant historical progress towards happiness or perfection or something, who feels very powerful because he feels connected to these forces, moving uphill all the time . . . maybe that person can't, um, incorporate sickness into his sense of how things are supposed to go. Maybe vomit . . . and sores and disease . . . really frighten him, maybe . . . he isn't so good with death.

RABBI ISIDOR CHEMELWITZ: The Holy Scriptures have nothing to say about such a person.

LOUIS: Rabbi, I'm afraid of the crimes I may commit.

RABBI ISIDOR CHEMELWITZ: Please, mister. I'm a sick old rabbi facing a long drive home to the Bronx. You want to confess, better you should find a priest.

LOUIS: But I'm not a Catholic, I'm a Jew.

RABBI ISIDOR CHEMELWITZ: Worse luck for you, bubbulah. Catholics believe in forgiveness. Jews believe in Guilt. *(He pats the coffin tenderly)*

LOUIS: You just make sure those pegs are in good and tight.

RABBI ISIDOR CHEMELWITZ: Don't worry, mister. The life she had, she'll stay put. She's better off.

JOE: Look, I know this is scary for you. But try to understand what it means to me. Will you try?

HARPER: Yes.

JOE: Good. Really try.

I think things are starting to change in the world.

HARPER: But I don't want . . .

JOE: Wait. For the good. Change for the good. America has rediscovered itself. Its sacred position among nations. And people aren't ashamed of that like they used to be. This is a great thing. The truth restored. Law restored. That's what President Reagan's done, Harper. He says "Truth exists and can be spoken proudly." And the country responds to him. We become better. More good. I need to be a part of that, I need something big to lift me up. I mean, six years ago the world seemed in decline, horrible, hopeless, full of unsolvable problems and crime and confusion and hunger and . . .

HARPER: But it still seems that way. More now than before. They say the ozone layer is . . .

JOE: Harper . . .

HARPER: And today out the window on Atlantic Avenue there was a schizophrenic traffic cop who was making these . . .

JOE: Stop it! I'm trying to make a point.

HARPER: So am I.

JOE: You aren't even making sense, you . . .

HARPER: My point is the world seems just as . . .

JOE: It only seems that way to you because you never go out in the world, Harper, and you have emotional problems.

HARPER: I do so get out in the world.

JOE: You don't. You stay in all day, fretting about imaginary . . .

HARPER: I get out. I do. You don't know what I do.

JOE: You don't stay in all day.

HARPER: No.

JOE: Well. . . . Yes you do.

HARPER: That's what you think.

JOE: Where do you go?

HARPER: Where do *you* go? When you walk.

    (Pause, then angrily) And I DO NOT have emotional problems.

JOE: I'm sorry.

HARPER: And if I do have emotional problems it's from living with you. Or . . .

JOE: I'm sorry buddy, I didn't mean to . . .

HARPER: Or if you do think I do then you should never have married me. You have all these secrets and lies.

JOE: I want to be married to you, Harper.

HARPER: You shouldn't. You never should.

    (Pause)

    Hey buddy. Hey buddy.

JOE: Buddy kiss . . .

(They kiss.)

HARPER: I heard on the radio how to give a blowjob.

JOE: What?

HARPER: You want to try?

JOE: You really shouldn't listen to stuff like that.

HARPER: Mormons can give blowjobs.

JOE: *Harper.*

HARPER *(Imitating his tone)*: *Joe.*

    It was a little Jewish lady with a German accent. This is a good time. For me to make a baby.

(Little pause. Joe turns away.)

HARPER: Then they went on to a program about holes in the ozone layer. Over Antarctica. Skin burns, birds go blind, icebergs melt. The world's coming to an end.

Scene 6

First week of November. In the men's room of the offices of the Brooklyn Federal Court of Appeals; Louis is crying over the sink; Joe enters.

JOE: Oh, um. . . . Morning.

LOUIS: Good morning, counselor.

JOE *(He watches Louis cry)*: Sorry, I . . . I don't know your name.

LOUIS: Don't bother. Word processor. The lowest of the low.

JOE *(Holding out hand)*: Joe Pitt. I'm with Justice Wilson . . .

LOUIS: Oh, I know that. Counselor Pitt. Chief Clerk.

JOE: Were you . . . are you OK?

LOUIS: Oh, yeah. Thanks. What a nice man.

JOE: Not so nice.

LOUIS: What?

JOE: Not so nice. Nothing. You sure you're . . .

LOUIS: Life sucks shit. Life . . . just sucks shit.

JOE: What's wrong?

LOUIS: Run in my nylons.

JOE: Sorry . . . ?

LOUIS: Forget it. Look, thanks for asking.

JOE: Well . . .

LOUIS: I mean it really is nice of you.
    (He starts crying again)
    Sorry, sorry, sick friend . . .

JOE: Oh, I'm sorry.

LOUIS: Yeah, yeah, well, that's sweet.

Three of your colleagues have preceded you to this baleful sight and you're the first one to ask. The others just opened the door, saw me, and fled. I hope they had to pee real bad.

JOE *(Handing him a wad of toilet paper)*: They just didn't want to intrude.

LOUIS: Hah. Reaganite heartless macho asshole lawyers.

JOE: Oh, that's unfair.

LOUIS: What is? Heartless? Macho? Reaganite? Lawyer?

JOE: I voted for Reagan.

LOUIS: You did?

JOE: Twice.

LOUIS: Twice? Well, oh boy. A Gay Republican.

JOE: Excuse me?

LOUIS: Nothing.

JOE: I'm not . . .

Forget it.

LOUIS: Republican? Not Republican? Or . . .

JOE: What?

LOUIS: What?

JOE: Not gay. I'm not gay.

LOUIS: Oh. Sorry.

(Blows his nose loudly) It's just . . .

JOE: Yes?

LOUIS: Well, sometimes you can tell from the way a person sounds that . . . I mean you *sound* like a . . .

JOE: No I don't. Like what?

LOUIS: Like a Republican.

(Little pause. Joe knows he's being teased; Louis knows he knows. Joe decides to be a little brave.)

JOE *(Making sure no one else is around)*: Do I? Sound like a . . . ?
LOUIS: What? Like a . . . ? Republican, or . . . ? Do *I*?
JOE: Do you what?
LOUIS: Sound like a . . . ?
JOE: Like a . . . ?

I'm . . . confused.
LOUIS: Yes.

My name is Louis. But all my friends call me Louise. I work in Word Processing. Thanks for the toilet paper.

(Louis offers Joe his hand, Joe reaches, Louis feints and pecks Joe on the cheek, then exits.)

Scene 7

A week later. Mutual dream scene. Prior is at a fantastic makeup table, having a dream, applying the face. Harper is having a pill-induced hallucination. She has these from time to time. For some reason, Prior has appeared in this one. Or Harper has appeared in Prior's dream. It is bewildering.

PRIOR *(Alone, putting on makeup, then examining the results in the mirror; to the audience)*: "I'm ready for my closeup, Mr. DeMille."

One wants to move through life with elegance and grace, blossoming infrequently but with exquisite taste, and perfect timing, like a rare bloom, a zebra orchid. . . . One wants. . . . But one so seldom gets what one wants, does one? No. One does not. One gets fucked. Over. One . . . dies at thirty, robbed of . . . decades of majesty.

Fuck this shit. Fuck this shit.

(He almost crumbles; he pulls himself together; he studies his handiwork in the mirror)

I look like a corpse. A corpsette. Oh my queen; you know you've hit rock-bottom when even drag is a drag.

(Harper appears.)

HARPER: Are you. . . . Who are you?

PRIOR: Who are you?

HARPER: What are you doing in my hallucination?

PRIOR: I'm not in your hallucination. You're in my dream.

HARPER: You're wearing makeup.

PRIOR: So are you.

HARPER: But you're a man.

PRIOR *(Feigning dismay, shock, he mimes slashing his throat with his lipstick and dies, fabulously tragic. Then)*: The hands and feet give it away.

HARPER: There must be some mistake here. I don't recognize you. You're not. . . . Are you my . . . some sort of imaginary friend?

PRIOR: No. Aren't you too old to have imaginary friends?

HARPER: I have emotional problems. I took too many pills. Why are you wearing makeup?

PRIOR: I was in the process of applying the face, trying to make myself feel better—I swiped the new fall colors at the Clinique counter at Macy's. *(Showing her)*

HARPER: You stole these?

PRIOR: I was out of cash; it was an emotional emergency!

HARPER: Joe will be so angry. I promised him. No more pills.

PRIOR: These pills you keep alluding to?

HARPER: Valium. I take Valium. Lots of Valium.

PRIOR: And you're dancing as fast as you can.

HARPER: I'm not *addicted*. I don't believe in addiction, and I never . . . well, I *never* drink. And I *never* take drugs.

PRIOR: Well, smell *you*, Nancy Drew.

HARPER: Except Valium.

PRIOR: Except Valium; in wee fistfuls.

HARPER: It's terrible. Mormons are not supposed to be addicted to anything. I'm a Mormon.

PRIOR: I'm a homosexual.

HARPER: Oh! In my church we don't believe in homosexuals.

PRIOR: In my church we don't believe in Mormons.

HARPER: What church do . . . oh! *(She laughs)* I get it.

I don't understand this. If I didn't ever see you before and I don't think I did then I don't think you should be here, in this hallucination, because in my experience the mind, which is where hallucinations come from, shouldn't be able to make up anything that wasn't there to start with, that didn't enter it from experience, from the real world. Imagination can't create anything new, can it? It only recycles bits and pieces from the world and reassembles them into visions. . . . Am I making sense right now?

PRIOR: Given the circumstances, yes.

HARPER: So when we think we've escaped the unbearable ordinariness and, well, untruthfulness of our lives, it's really only the same old ordinariness and falseness rearranged into the appearance of novelty and truth. Nothing unknown is knowable. Don't you think it's depressing?

PRIOR: The limitations of the imagination?

HARPER: Yes.

PRIOR: It's something you learn after your second theme party: It's All Been Done Before.

HARPER: The world. Finite. Terribly, terribly. . . . Well . . .

This is the most depressing hallucination I've ever had.

PRIOR: Apologies. I do try to be amusing.

HARPER: Oh, well, don't apologize, you. . . . I can't expect someone who's really sick to entertain me.

PRIOR: How on earth did you know . . .

HARPER: Oh that happens. This is the very threshold of revelation sometimes. You can see things . . . how sick you are. Do you see anything about me?

PRIOR: Yes.

HARPER: What?

PRIOR: You are amazingly unhappy.

HARPER: Oh big deal. You meet a Valium addict and you figure out she's unhappy. That doesn't count. Of course I. . . . Something else. Something surprising.

PRIOR: Something surprising.

HARPER: Yes.

PRIOR: Your husband's a homo.

(Pause.)

HARPER: Oh, ridiculous.

(Pause, then very quietly)

Really?

PRIOR *(Shrugs)*: Threshold of revelation.

HARPER: Well I don't like your revelations. I don't think you intuit well at all. Joe's a very normal man, he . . .

Oh God. Oh God. He. . . . Do homos take, like, lots of long walks?

PRIOR: Yes. We do. In stretch pants with lavender coifs. I just looked at you, and there was . . .

HARPER: A sort of blue streak of recognition.

PRIOR: Yes.

HARPER: Like you knew me incredibly well.

PRIOR: Yes.

HARPER: Yes.

I have to go now, get back, something just . . . fell apart.

Oh God, I feel so sad . . .

PRIOR: I . . . I'm sorry. I usually say, "Fuck the truth," but mostly, the truth fucks you.

HARPER: I see something else about you . . .

PRIOR: Oh?

HARPER: Deep inside you, there's a part of you, the most inner part, entirely free of disease. I can see that.

PRIOR: Is that. . . . That isn't true.

HARPER: Threshhold of revelation.

Home . . .

(She vanishes.)

PRIOR: People come and g<u>o</u> so quickly here . . .

(To himself in the mirror) I don't think there's any uninfected part of me. My heart is pumping polluted blood. I feel dirty.

(He begins to wipe makeup off with his hands, smearing it around. A large gray feather falls from up above. Prior stops smearing the makeup and looks at the feather. He goes to it and picks it up.)

A VOICE *(It is an incredibly beautiful voice)*: Look up!

PRIOR *(Looking up, not seeing anyone)*: Hello?

A VOICE: Look up!

PRIOR: Who is that?

A VOICE: Prepare the way!

PRIOR: I don't see any . . .

(There is a dramatic change in lighting, from above.)

A VOICE:

> Look up, look up,
> prepare the way
> the infinite descent
> A breath in air
> floating down
> Glory to . . .

(Silence.)

PRIOR: Hello? Is that it? Helloooo!

What the fuck . . . ? *(He holds himself)*

Poor me. Poor poor me. Why me? Why poor poor me? Oh I don't feel good right now. I really don't.

Scene 8

That night. Split scene: Harper and Joe at home; Prior and Louis in bed.

HARPER: Where were you?

JOE: Out.

HARPER: Where?

JOE: Just out. Thinking.

HARPER: It's late.

JOE: I had a lot to think about.

HARPER: I burned dinner.

JOE: Sorry.

HARPER: Not my dinner. My dinner was fine. Your dinner. I put it back in the oven and turned everything up as high as it could go and I watched till it burned black. It's still hot. Very hot. Want it?

JOE: You didn't have to do that.

HARPER: I know. It just seemed like the kind of thing a mentally deranged sex-starved pill-popping housewife would do.

JOE: Uh huh.

HARPER: So I did it. Who knows anymore what I have to do?

JOE: How many pills?

HARPER: A bunch. Don't change the subject.

JOE: I won't talk to you when you . . .

HARPER: No. No. Don't do that! I'm . . . I'm fine, pills are not the problem, not our problem, I WANT TO KNOW WHERE YOU'VE BEEN! I WANT TO KNOW WHAT'S GOING ON!

JOE: Going on with what? The job?

HARPER: Not the job.

JOE: I said I need more time.

HARPER: Not the job!

JOE: Mr. Cohn, I talked to him on the phone, he said I had to hurry . . .

HARPER: Not the . . .

JOE: But I can't get you to talk sensibly about anything so . . .

HARPER: SHUT UP!

JOE: Then what?

HARPER: Stick to the subject.

JOE: I don't know what that is. You have something you want to ask me? Ask me. Go.

HARPER: I . . . can't. I'm scared of you.

JOE: I'm tired, I'm going to bed.

HARPER: Tell me without making me ask. Please.

JOE: This is crazy, I'm not . . .

HARPER: When you come through the door at night your face is never exactly the way I remembered it. I get surprised by something . . . mean and hard about the way you look. Even the weight of you in the bed at night, the way you breathe in your sleep seems unfamiliar.

> You terrify me.

JOE *(Cold)*: I know who you are.

HARPER: Yes. I'm the enemy. That's easy. That doesn't change.

> You think you're the only one who hates sex; I do; I hate it with you; I do. I dream that you batter away at me till all my joints come apart, like wax, and I fall into pieces. It's like a punishment. It was wrong of me to marry you. I knew you . . . *(She stops herself)* It's a sin, and it's killing us both.

JOE: I can always tell when you've taken pills because it makes you red-faced and sweaty and frankly that's very often why I don't want to . . .

HARPER: Because . . .

JOE: Well, you aren't pretty. Not like this.

HARPER: I have something to ask you.

JOE: Then ASK! ASK! What in hell are you . . .

HARPER: Are you a homo?

> *(Pause)*

> Are you? If you try to walk out right now I'll put your dinner back in the oven and turn it up so high the whole

building will fill with smoke and everyone in it will as-
phyxiate. So help me God I will.

Now answer the question.

JOE: What if I . . .

(Small pause.)

HARPER: Then tell me, please. And we'll see.

JOE: No. I'm not.

I don't see what difference it makes.

LOUIS: Jews don't have any clear textual guide to the afterlife;
even that it exists. I don't think much about it. I see it as
a perpetual rainy Thursday afternoon in March. Dead
leaves.

PRIOR: Eeeugh. Very Greco-Roman.

LOUIS: Well for us it's not the verdict that counts, it's the act of
judgment. That's why I could never be a lawyer. In court
all that matters is the verdict.

PRIOR: You could never be a lawyer because you are oversexed.
You're too distracted.

LOUIS: Not distracted; *ab*stracted. I'm trying to make a point:

PRIOR: Namely:

LOUIS: It's the judge in his or her chambers, weighing, books
open, pondering the evidence, ranging freely over catego-
ries: good, evil, innocent, guilty; the judge in the chamber of circumspection, not the judge on the bench with
the gavel. The shaping of the law, not its execution.

PRIOR: The point, dear, the point . . .

LOUIS: That it should be the questions and shape of a life,
its total complexity gathered, arranged and considered,
which matters in the end, not some stamp of salvation
or damnation which disperses all the complexity in

some unsatisfying little decision—the balancing of the scales . . .

PRIOR: I like this; very zen; it's . . . reassuringly incomprehensible and useless. We who are about to die thank you.

LOUIS: You are not about to die.

PRIOR: It's not going well, really . . . two new lesions. My leg hurts. There's protein in my urine, the doctor says, but who knows what the fuck that portends. Anyway it shouldn't be there, the protein. My butt is chapped from diarrhea and yesterday I shat blood.

LOUIS: I really hate this. You don't tell me . . .

PRIOR: You get too upset, I wind up comforting you. It's easier . . .

LOUIS: Oh thanks.

PRIOR: If it's bad I'll tell you.

LOUIS: Shitting blood sounds bad to me.

PRIOR: And I'm telling you.

LOUIS: And I'm handling it.

PRIOR: Tell me some more about justice.

LOUIS: I *am* handling it.

PRIOR: Well Louis you win Trooper of the Month.

(Louis starts to cry.)

PRIOR: I take it back. You aren't Trooper of the Month.
     This isn't working . . .
     Tell me some more about justice.

LOUIS: You are not about to die.

PRIOR: Justice . . .

LOUIS: . . . is an immensity, a confusing vastness. Justice is God.
     Prior?

PRIOR: Hmmm?

LOUIS: You love me.

PRIOR: Yes.

LOUIS: What if I walked out on this?

Would you hate me forever?

(Prior kisses Louis on the forehead.)

PRIOR: Yes.

JOE: I think we ought to pray. Ask God for help. Ask him together . . .

HARPER: God won't talk to me. I have to make up people to talk to me.

JOE: You have to keep asking.

HARPER: I forgot the question.

Oh yeah. God, is my husband a . . .

JOE *(Scary)*: Stop it. Stop it. I'm warning you.

Does it make any difference? That I might be one thing deep within, no matter how wrong or ugly that thing is, so long as I have fought, with everything I have, to kill it. What do you want from me? What do you want from me, Harper? More than that? For God's sake, there's nothing left, I'm a shell. There's nothing left to kill.

As long as my behavior is what I know it has to be. Decent. Correct. That alone in the eyes of God.

HARPER: No, no, not that, that's Utah talk, Mormon talk, I hate it, Joe, tell me, say it . . .

JOE: All I will say is that I am a very good man who has worked very hard to become good and you want to destroy that. You want to destroy me, but I am not going to let you do that.

(Pause.)

HARPER: I'm going to have a baby.

JOE: Liar.

HARPER: You liar.

A baby born addicted to pills. A baby who does not dream but who hallucinates, who stares up at us with big mirror eyes and who does not know who we are.

(Pause.)

JOE: Are you really . . .

HARPER: No. Yes. No. Yes. Get away from me.

Now we both have a secret.

PRIOR: One of my ancestors was a ship's captain who made money bringing whale oil to Europe and returning with immigrants—Irish mostly, packed in tight, so many dollars per head. The last ship he captained foundered off the coast of Nova Scotia in a winter tempest and sank to the bottom. He went down with the ship—la Grande Geste—but his crew took seventy women and kids in the ship's only longboat, this big, open rowboat, and when the weather got too rough, and they thought the boat was overcrowded, the crew started lifting people up and hurling them into the sea. Until they got the ballast right. They walked up and down the longboat, eyes to the waterline, and when the boat rode low in the water they'd grab the nearest passenger and throw them into the sea. The boat was leaky, see; seventy people; they arrived in Halifax with nine people on board.

LOUIS: Jesus.

PRIOR: I think about that story a lot now. People in a boat, waiting, terrified, while implacable, unsmiling men, irresistibly strong, seize . . . maybe the person next to you, maybe you, and with no warning at all, with time only for a quick intake of air you are pitched into freezing, turbulent water and salt and darkness to drown.

I like your cosmology, baby. While time is running out I find myself drawn to anything that's suspended, that lacks an ending—but it seems to me that it lets you off scot-free.

LOUIS: What do you mean?

PRIOR: No judgment, no guilt or responsibility.

LOUIS: For me.

PRIOR: For anyone. It was an editorial "you."

LOUIS: Please get better. Please.

Please don't get any sicker.

Scene 9

Third week in November. Roy and Henry, his doctor, in Henry's office.

HENRY: Nobody knows what causes it. And nobody knows how to cure it. The best theory is that we blame a retrovirus, the Human Immunodeficiency Virus. Its presence is made known to us by the useless antibodies which appear in reaction to its entrance into the bloodstream through a cut, or an orifice. The antibodies are powerless to protect the body against it. Why, we don't know. The body's immune system ceases to function. Sometimes the body even attacks itself. At any rate it's left open to a whole horror house of infections from microbes which it usually defends against.

Like Kaposi's sarcomas. These lesions. Or your throat problem. Or the glands.

We think it may also be able to slip past the blood-brain barrier into the brain. Which is of course very bad news.

And it's fatal in we don't know what percent of people with suppressed immune responses.

(Pause.)

ROY: This is very interesting, Mr. Wizard, but why the fuck are you telling me this?

(Pause.)

HENRY: Well, I have just removed one of three lesions which biopsy results will probably tell us is a Kaposi's sarcoma lesion. And you have a pronounced swelling of glands in your neck, groin, and armpits—lymphadenopathy is another sign. And you have oral candidiasis and maybe a little more fungus under the fingernails of two digits on your right hand. So that's why . . .

ROY: This disease . . .

HENRY: Syndrome.

ROY: Whatever. It afflicts mostly homosexuals and drug addicts.

HENRY: Mostly. Hemophiliacs are also at risk.

ROY: Homosexuals and drug addicts. So why are you implying that I . . .

(Pause)

What are you implying, Henry?

HENRY: I don't . . .

ROY: I'm not a drug addict.

HENRY: Oh come on Roy.

ROY: What, what, come on Roy what? Do you think I'm a junkie, Henry, do you see tracks?

HENRY: This is absurd.

ROY: Say it.

HENRY: Say what?

ROY: Say, "Roy Cohn, you are a . . ."

HENRY: Roy.

ROY: "You are a. . . ." Go on. Not "Roy Cohn you are a drug fiend." "Roy Marcus Cohn, you are a . . ."

Go on, Henry, it starts with an "H."

HENRY: Oh I'm not going to . . .

ROY: *With an "H,"* Henry, and it isn't "Hemophiliac." Come on . . .

HENRY: What are you doing, Roy?

ROY: No, say it. I mean it. Say: "Roy Cohn, you are a homosexual."

(Pause)

And I will proceed, systematically, to destroy your reputation and your practice and your career in New York State, Henry. Which you know I can do.

(Pause.)

HENRY: Roy, you have been seeing me since 1958. Apart from the facelifts I have treated you for everything from syphilis . . .

ROY: From a whore in Dallas.

HENRY: From syphilis to venereal warts. In your rectum. Which you may have gotten from a whore in Dallas, but it wasn't a female whore.

(Pause.)

ROY: So say it.

HENRY: Roy Cohn, you are . . .

You have had sex with men, many many times, Roy, and one of them, or any number of them, has made you very sick. You have AIDS.

ROY: AIDS.

Your problem, Henry, is that you are hung up on words, on labels, that you believe they mean what they seem to mean. AIDS. Homosexual. Gay. Lesbian. You think these are names that tell you who someone sleeps with, but they don't tell you that.

HENRY: No?

ROY: No. Like all labels they tell you one thing and one thing only: where does an individual so identified fit in the food chain, in the pecking order? Not ideology, or sexual taste, but something much simpler: clout. Not who I fuck or who fucks me, but who will pick up the phone when I call, who owes me favors. This is what a label refers to. Now to someone who does not understand this, homosexual is what I am because I have sex with men. But really this is wrong. Homosexuals are not men who sleep with other men. Homosexuals are men who in fifteen years of trying cannot get a pissant antidiscrimination bill through City Council. Homosexuals are men who know nobody and who nobody knows. Who have zero clout. Does this sound like me, Henry?

HENRY: No.

ROY: No. I have clout. A lot. I can pick up this phone, punch fifteen numbers, and you know who will be on the other end in under five minutes, Henry?

HENRY: The President.

ROY: Even better, Henry. His wife.

HENRY: I'm impressed.

ROY: I don't want you to be impressed. I want you to understand. This is not sophistry. And this is not hypocrisy.
This is reality. I have sex with men. But unlike nearly
every other man of whom this is true, I bring the guy I'm
screwing to the White House and President Reagan
smiles at us and shakes his hand. Because *what* I am is
defined entirely by *who* I am. Roy Cohn is not a homosexual. Roy Cohn is a heterosexual man, Henry, who
fucks around with guys.

HENRY: OK, Roy.

ROY: And what is my diagnosis, Henry?

HENRY: You have AIDS, Roy.

ROY: No, Henry, no. AIDS is what homosexuals have. I have
liver cancer.

(Pause.)

HENRY: Well, whatever the fuck you have, Roy, it's very serious,
and I haven't got a damn thing for you. The NIH in
Bethesda has a new drug called AZT with a two-year
waiting list that not even I can get you onto. So get on the
phone, Roy, and dial the fifteen numbers, and tell the First
Lady you need in on an experimental treatment for liver
cancer, because you can call it any damn thing you want,
Roy, but what it boils down to is very bad news.

ACT TWO:

In Vitro

December 1985–January 1986

Scene 1

Night, the third week in December. Prior alone on the floor of his bedroom; he is much worse.

PRIOR: Louis, Louis, please wake up, oh God.

(Louis runs in.)

PRIOR: I think something horrible is wrong with me I can't breathe . . .

LOUIS *(Starting to exit)*: I'm calling the ambulance.

PRIOR: No, wait, I . . .

LOUIS: *Wait?* Are you fucking crazy? Oh God you're on fire, your head is on fire.

PRIOR: It hurts, it hurts . . .

LOUIS: I'm calling the ambulance.

PRIOR: I don't want to go to the hospital, I don't want to go to the hospital please let me lie here, just . . .

53

LOUIS: No, no, God, Prior, stand up . . .

PRIOR: DON'T TOUCH MY LEG!

LOUIS: We have to . . . oh God this is so crazy.

PRIOR: I'll be OK if I just lie here Lou, really, if I can only sleep a little . . .

(Louis exits.)

PRIOR: Louis?

NO! NO! Don't call, you'll send me there and I won't come back, please, please Louis I'm begging, baby, please . . .

(Screams) LOUIS!!

LOUIS *(From off; hysterical)*: WILL YOU SHUT THE FUCK UP!

PRIOR *(Trying to stand)*: Aaaah. I have . . . to go to the bathroom. Wait. Wait, just . . . oh. Oh God. *(He shits himself)*

LOUIS *(Entering)*: Prior? They'll be here in . . .

Oh my God.

PRIOR: I'm sorry, I'm sorry.

LOUIS: What did . . . ? What?

PRIOR: I had an accident.

(Louis goes to him.)

LOUIS: This is blood.

PRIOR: Maybe you shouldn't touch it . . . me. . . . I . . . *(He faints)*

LOUIS *(Quietly)*: Oh help. Oh help. Oh God oh God oh God help me I can't I can't I can't.

Scene 2

Same night. Harper is sitting at home, all alone, with no lights on. We can barely see her. Joe enters, but he doesn't turn on the lights.

JOE: Why are you sitting in the dark? Turn on the light.

HARPER: *No.* I heard the sounds in the bedroom again. I know someone was in there.

JOE: No one was.

HARPER: Maybe actually in the bed, under the covers with a knife.

Oh, boy. Joe. I, um, I'm thinking of going away. By which I mean: I think I'm going off again. You . . . you know what I mean?

JOE: Please don't. Stay. We can fix it. I pray for that. This is my fault, but I can correct it. You have to try too . . .

(He turns on the light. She turns it off again.)

HARPER: When you pray, what do you pray for?

JOE: I pray for God to crush me, break me up into little pieces and start all over again.

HARPER: Oh. Please. Don't pray for that.

JOE: I had a book of Bible stories when I was a kid. There was a picture I'd look at twenty times every day: Jacob wrestles with the angel. I don't really remember the story, or why the wrestling—just the picture. Jacob is young and very strong. The angel is . . . a beautiful man, with golden hair and wings, of course. I still dream about it. Many nights. I'm. . . . It's me. In that struggle. Fierce, and unfair. The angel is not human, and it holds nothing back, so how

55

could anyone human win, what kind of a fight is that? It's not just. Losing means your soul thrown down in the dust, your heart torn out from God's. But you can't not lose.

HARPER: In the whole entire world, you are the only person, the only person I love or have ever loved. And I love you terribly. Terribly. That's what's so awfully, irreducibly real. I can make up anything but I can't dream that away.

JOE: Are you . . . are you really going to have a baby?

HARPER: It's my time, and there's no blood. I don't really know. I suppose it wouldn't be a great thing. Maybe I'm just not bleeding because I take too many pills. Maybe I'll give birth to a pill. That would give a new meaning to pill-popping, huh?

I think you should go to Washington. Alone. Change, like you said.

JOE: I'm not going to leave you, Harper.

HARPER: Well maybe not. But I'm going to leave you.

Scene 3

One AM, the next morning. Louis and a nurse, Emily, are sitting in Prior's room in the hospital.

EMILY: He'll be all right now.

LOUIS: No he won't.

EMILY: No. I guess not. I gave him something that makes him sleep.

LOUIS: Deep asleep?

EMILY: Orbiting the moons of Jupiter.

LOUIS: A good place to be.

EMILY: Anyplace better than here. You his . . . uh?

LOUIS: Yes. I'm his uh.

EMILY: This must be hell for you.

LOUIS: It is. Hell. The After Life. Which is not at all like a rainy afternoon in March, by the way, Prior. A lot more vivid than I'd expected. Dead leaves, but the crunchy kind. Sharp, dry air. The kind of long, luxurious dying feeling that breaks your heart.

EMILY: Yeah, well we all get to break our hearts on this one.
     He seems like a nice guy. Cute.

LOUIS: Not like this.
     Yes, he is. Was. Whatever.

EMILY: Weird name. Prior Walter. Like, "The Walter before this one."

LOUIS: Lots of Walters before this one. Prior is an old old family name in an old old family. The Walters go back to the Mayflower and beyond. Back to the Norman Conquest. He says there's a Prior Walter stitched into the Bayeux tapestry.

EMILY: Is that impressive?

LOUIS: Well, it's old. Very old. Which in some circles equals impressive.

EMILY: Not in my circle. What's the name of the tapestry?

LOUIS: The Bayeux tapestry. Embroidered by La Reine Mathilde.

EMILY: I'll tell my mother. She embroiders. Drives me nuts.

LOUIS: Manual therapy for anxious hands.

EMILY: Maybe you should try it.

LOUIS: Mathilde stitched while William the Conqueror was off to war. She was capable of . . . more than loyalty. Devotion.
     She waited for him, she stitched for years. And if he had come back broken and defeated from war, she would

have loved him even more. And if he had returned muti-
lated, ugly, full of infection and horror, she would still
have loved him; fed by pity, by a sharing of pain, she
would love him even more, and even more, and she would
never, never have prayed to God, please let him die if he
can't return to me whole and healthy and able to live a
normal life. . . . If he had died, she would have buried her
heart with him.

So what the fuck is the matter with me?

(Little pause)

Will he sleep through the night?

EMILY: At least.

LOUIS: I'm going.

EMILY: It's one AM. Where do you have to go at . . .

LOUIS: I know what time it is. A walk. Night air, good for
the. . . . The park.

EMILY: Be careful.

LOUIS: Yeah. Danger.

Tell him, if he wakes up and you're still on, tell him
goodbye, tell him I had to go.

Scene 4

*An hour later. Split scene: Joe and Roy in a fancy (straight)
bar; Louis and a Man in the Ramble in Central Park. Joe
and Roy are sitting at the bar; the place is brightly lit. Joe has
a plate of food in front of him but he isn't eating. Roy occasionally reaches over the table and forks small bites off Joe's
plate. Roy is in a tuxedo, bow tie loosened; Joe is dressed casu-
ally. Roy is drinking heavily, Joe not at all. Louis and the
Man are eyeing each other, each alternating interest and
indifference.*

JOE: The pills were something she started when she miscarried or . . . no, she took some before that. She had a really bad time at home, when she was a kid, her home was really bad. I think a lot of drinking and physical stuff. She doesn't talk about that, instead she talks about . . . the sky falling down, people with knives hiding under sofas. Monsters. Mormons. Everyone thinks Mormons don't come from homes like that, we aren't supposed to behave that way, but we do. It's not lying, or being two-faced. Everyone tries very hard to live up to God's strictures, which are very . . . um . . .

ROY: Strict.

JOE: I shouldn't be bothering you with this.

ROY: No, please. Heart to heart. Want another. . . . What is that, seltzer?

JOE: The failure to measure up hits people very hard. From such a strong desire to be good they feel very far from goodness when they fail.

What scares me is that maybe what I really love in her is the part of her that's farthest from the light, from God's love; maybe I was drawn to that in the first place. And I'm keeping it alive because I need it.

ROY: Why would you need it?

JOE: There are things. . . . I don't know how well we know ourselves. I mean, what if? I know I married her because she . . . because I loved it that she was always wrong, always doing something wrong, like one step out of step. In Salt Lake City that stands out. I never stood out, on the outside, but inside, it was hard for me. To pass.

ROY: Pass?

JOE: Yeah.

ROY: Pass as what?

JOE: Oh. Well. . . . As someone cheerful and strong. Those who love God with an open heart unclouded by secrets and struggles are cheerful; God's easy simple love for them shows in how strong and happy they are. The saints.

ROY: But you had secrets? Secret struggles . . .

JOE: I wanted to be one of the elect, one of the Blessed. You feel you ought to be, that the blemishes are yours by choice, which of course they aren't. Harper's sorrow, that really deep sorrow, she didn't choose that. But it's there.

ROY: You didn't put it there.

JOE: No.

ROY: You sound like you think you did.

JOE: I am responsible for her.

ROY: Because she's your wife.

JOE: That. And I do love her.

ROY: Whatever. She's your wife. And so there are obligations. To her. But also to yourself.

JOE: She'd fall apart in Washington.

ROY: Then let her stay here.

JOE: She'll fall apart if I leave her.

ROY: Then bring her to Washington.

JOE: I just can't, Roy. She needs me.

ROY: Listen, Joe. I'm the best divorce lawyer in the business.

(Little pause.)

JOE: Can't Washington wait?

ROY: You do what you need to do, Joe. What *you* need. *You.* Let her life go where it wants to go. You'll both be better for that. *Somebody* should get what they want.

MAN: What do you want?

LOUIS: I want you to fuck me, hurt me, make me bleed.

MAN: I want to.

LOUIS: Yeah?

MAN: I want to hurt you.

LOUIS: Fuck me.

MAN: Yeah?

LOUIS: Hard.

MAN: Yeah? You been a bad boy?

(Pause. Louis laughs, softly.)

LOUIS: Very bad. Very bad.

MAN: You need to be punished, boy?

LOUIS: Yes. I do.

MAN: Yes what?

(Little pause.)

LOUIS: Um, I . . .

MAN: Yes *what*, boy?

LOUIS: Oh. Yes sir.

MAN: I want you to take me to your place, boy.

LOUIS: No, I can't do that.

MAN: No *what*?

LOUIS: No sir, I can't, I . . .

I don't live alone, sir.

MAN: Your lover know you're out with a man tonight, boy?

LOUIS: No sir, he . . .

My lover doesn't know.

MAN: Your lover know you . . .

LOUIS: Let's change the subject, OK? Can we go to your place?

MAN: I live with my parents.

LOUIS: Oh.

ROY: Everyone who makes it in this world makes it because somebody older and more powerful takes an interest. The most precious asset in life, I think, is the ability to be a good son. You have that, Joe. Somebody who can be a good son to a father who pushes them farther than they would otherwise go. I've had many fathers, I owe my life to them, powerful, powerful men. Walter Winchell, Edgar Hoover. Joe McCarthy most of all. He valued me because I am a good lawyer, but he loved me because I was and am a good son. He was a very difficult man, very guarded and cagey; I brought out something tender in him. He would have died for me. And me for him. Does this embarrass you?

JOE: I had a hard time with my father.

ROY: Well sometimes that's the way. Then you have to find other fathers, substitutes, I don't know. The father-son relationship is central to life. Women are for birth, beginning, but the father is continuance. The son offers the father his life as a vessel for carrying forth his father's dream. Your father's living?

JOE: Um, dead.

ROY: He was . . . what? A difficult man?

JOE: He was in the military. He could be very unfair. And cold.

ROY: But he loved you.

JOE: I don't know.

ROY: No, no, Joe, he did, I know this. Sometimes a father's love has to be very, very hard, unfair even, cold to make his son grow strong in a world like this. This isn't a good world.

MAN: Here, then.

LOUIS: I. . . . Do you have a rubber?

MAN: I don't use rubbers.

LOUIS: You should. *(He takes one from his coat pocket)* Here.

MAN: I don't use them.

LOUIS: Forget it, then. *(He starts to leave)*

MAN: No, wait.

> Put it on me. Boy.

LOUIS: Forget it, I have to get back. Home. I must be going crazy.

MAN: Oh come on please he won't find out.

LOUIS: It's cold. Too cold.

MAN: It's never too cold, let me warm you up. Please?

(They begin to fuck.)

MAN: Relax.

LOUIS *(A small laugh)*: Not a chance.

MAN: It . . .

LOUIS: What?

MAN: I think it broke. The rubber. You want me to keep going?
(Little pause) Pull out? Should I . . .

LOUIS: Keep going.

> Infect me.
> I don't care. I don't care.

(Pause. The Man pulls out.)

MAN: I . . . um, look, I'm sorry, but I think I want to go.

LOUIS: Yeah.

> Give my best to mom and dad.

(The Man slaps him.)

LOUIS: Ow!

(They stare at each other.)

LOUIS: It was a joke.

(The Man leaves.)

ROY: How long have we known each other?

JOE: Since 1980.

ROY: Right. A long time. I feel close to you, Joe. Do I advise you well?

JOE: You've been an incredible friend, Roy, I . . .

ROY: I want to be family. Familia, as my Italian friends call it. La Familia. A lovely word. It's important for me to help you, like I was helped.

JOE: I owe practically everything to you, Roy.

ROY: I'm dying, Joe. Cancer.

JOE: Oh my God.

ROY: Please. Let me finish.

Few people know this and I'm telling you this only because. . . . I'm not afraid of death. What can death bring that I haven't faced? I've lived; life is the worst. *(Gently mocking himself)* Listen to me, I'm a philosopher.

Joe. You must do this. You must must must. Love; that's a trap. Responsibility; that's a trap too. Like a father to a son I tell you this: Life is full of horror; nobody escapes, nobody; save yourself. Whatever pulls on you, whatever needs from you, threatens you. Don't be afraid; people are so afraid; don't be afraid to live in the raw wind, naked, alone. . . . Learn at least this: What you are capable of. Let nothing stand in your way.

Scene 5

Three days later. Prior and Belize in Prior's hospital room. Prior is very sick but improving. Belize has just arrived.

PRIOR: Miss Thing.

BELIZE: Ma cherie bichette.

PRIOR: Stella.

BELIZE: Stella for star. Let me see. *(Scrutinizing Prior)* You look like shit, why yes indeed you do, comme la merde!

PRIOR: Merci.

BELIZE *(Taking little plastic bottles from his bag, handing them to Prior)*: Not to despair, Belle Reeve. Lookie! Magic goop!

PRIOR *(Opening a bottle, sniffing)*: Pooh! What kinda crap is that?

BELIZE: Beats me. Let's rub it on your poor blistered body and see what it does.

PRIOR: This is not Western medicine, these bottles . . .

BELIZE: Voodoo cream. From the botanica 'round the block.

PRIOR: And you a registered nurse.

BELIZE *(Sniffing it)*: Beeswax and cheap perfume. Cut with Jergen's Lotion. Full of good vibes and love from some little black Cubana witch in Miami.

PRIOR: Get that trash away from me, I am immune-suppressed.

BELIZE: I *am* a health professional. I *know* what I'm doing.

PRIOR: It stinks. Any word from Louis?

(Pause. Belize starts giving Prior a gentle massage.)

PRIOR: Gone.

BELIZE: He'll be back. I know the type. Likes to keep a girl on edge.

PRIOR: It's been . . .

(Pause.)

BELIZE *(Trying to jog his memory)*: How long?

PRIOR: I don't remember.

BELIZE: How long have you been here?

PRIOR *(Getting suddenly upset)*: I don't remember, I don't give a fuck. I want Louis. I want my fucking boyfriend, where the fuck is he? I'm dying, I'm dying, where's Louis?

BELIZE: Shhhh, shhh . . .

PRIOR: This is a very strange drug, this drug. Emotional lability, for starters.

BELIZE: Save a tab or two for me.

PRIOR: Oh no, not this drug, ce n'est pas pour la joyeux noël et la bonne année, this drug she is serious poisonous chemistry, ma pauvre bichette.

And not just disorienting. I hear things. Voices.

BELIZE: Voices.

PRIOR: A voice.

BELIZE: Saying what?

(Pause.)

PRIOR: I'm not supposed to tell.

BELIZE: You better tell the doctor. Or I will.

PRIOR: No no don't. Please. I want the voice; it's wonderful. It's all that's keeping me alive. I don't want to talk to some intern about it.

You know what happens? When I hear it, I get hard.

BELIZE: Oh my.

PRIOR: Comme ça. *(He uses his arm to demonstrate)* And you know I am slow to rise.

BELIZE: My jaw aches at the memory.

PRIOR: And would you deny me this little solace—betray my concupiscence to Florence Nightingale's storm troopers?

BELIZE: Perish the thought, ma bébé.

PRIOR: They'd change the drug just to spoil the fun.

BELIZE: You and your boner can depend on me.

PRIOR: Je t'adore, ma belle nègre.

BELIZE: All this girl-talk shit is politically incorrect, you know. We should have dropped it back when we gave up drag.

PRIOR: I'm sick, I get to be politically incorrect if it makes me feel better. You sound like Lou.

> *(Little pause)*

> Well, at least I have the satisfaction of knowing he's in anguish somewhere. I loved his anguish. Watching him stick his head up his asshole and eat his guts out over some relatively minor moral conundrum—it was the best show in town. But Mother warned me: if they get overwhelmed by the little things . . .

BELIZE: They'll be belly-up bustville when something big comes along.

PRIOR: Mother warned me.

BELIZE: And they do come along.

PRIOR: But I didn't listen.

BELIZE: No. *(Doing Hepburn)* Men are beasts.

PRIOR *(Also Hepburn)*: The absolute lowest.

BELIZE: I have to go. If I want to spend my whole lonely life looking after white people I can get underpaid to do it.

PRIOR: You're just a Christian martyr.

BELIZE: Whatever happens, baby, I will be here for you.

PRIOR: Je t'aime.

BELIZE: Je t'aime. Don't go crazy on me, girlfriend, I already got enough crazy queens for one lifetime. For two. I can't be bothering with dementia.

PRIOR: I promise.

BELIZE *(Touching him; softly)*: Ouch.

PRIOR: Ouch. Indeed.

BELIZE: Why'd .they have to pick on you?

And eat more, girlfriend, you really do look like shit.

(Belize leaves.)

PRIOR *(After waiting a beat)*: He's gone.

Are you still . . .

VOICE: I can't stay. I will return.

PRIOR: Are you one of those "Follow me to the other side" voices?

VOICE: No. I am no nightbird. I am a messenger . . .

PRIOR: You have a beautiful voice, it sounds . . . like a viola, like a perfectly tuned, tight string, balanced, the truth. . . . Stay with me.

VOICE: Not now. Soon I will return, I will reveal myself to you; I am glorious, glorious; my heart, my countenance and my message. You must prepare.

PRIOR: For what? I don't want to . . .

VOICE: No death, no:

A marvelous work and a wonder we undertake, an edifice awry we sink plumb and straighten, a great Lie we abolish, a great error correct, with the rule, sword and broom of Truth!

PRIOR: What are you talking about, I . . .

VOICE:

I am on my way; when I am manifest, our Work begins:
Prepare for the parting of the air,
The breath, the ascent,
Glory to . . .

Scene 6

The second week of January. Martin, Roy and Joe in a fancy Manhattan restaurant.

MARTIN: It's a revolution in Washington, Joe. We have a new agenda and finally a real leader. They got back the Senate but we have the courts. By the nineties the Supreme Court will be block-solid Republican appointees, and the Federal bench—Republican judges like land mines, everywhere, everywhere they turn. Affirmative action? Take it to court. Boom! Land mine. And we'll get our way on just about everything: abortion, defense, Central America, family values, a live investment climate. We have the White House locked till the year 2000. And beyond. A permanent fix on the Oval Office? It's possible. By '92 we'll get the Senate back, and in ten years the South is going to give us the House. It's really the end of Liberalism. The end of New Deal Socialism. The end of ipso facto secular humanism. The dawning of a genuinely American political personality. Modeled on Ronald Wilson Reagan.

JOE: It sounds great, Mr. Heller.

MARTIN: Martin. And Justice is the hub. Especially since Ed Meese took over. He doesn't specialize in Fine Points of the Law. He's a flatfoot, a cop. He reminds me of Teddy Roosevelt.

JOE: I can't wait to meet him.

MARTIN: Too bad, Joe, he's been dead for sixty years!

(There is a little awkwardness. Joe doesn't respond.)

MARTIN: Teddy Roosevelt. You said you wanted to. . . . Little joke. It reminds me of the story about the . . .

69

ROY (*Smiling, but nasty*): Aw shut the fuck up Martin.

(*To Joe*) You see that? Mr. Heller here is one of the mighty, Joseph, in D.C. he sitteth on the right hand of the man who sitteth on the right hand of The Man. And yet I can say "shut the fuck up" and he will take no offense. Loyalty. He . . .

Martin?

MARTIN: Yes, Roy?

ROY: Rub my back.

MARTIN: Roy . . .

ROY: No no really, a sore spot, I get them all the time now, these. . . . Rub it for me darling, would you do that for me?

(*Martin rubs Roy's back. They both look at Joe.*)

ROY (*To Joe*): How do you think a handful of Bolsheviks turned St. Petersburg into Leningrad in one afternoon? *Comrades.* Who do for each other. Marx and Engels. Lenin and Trotsky. Josef Stalin and Franklin Delano Roosevelt.

(*Martin laughs.*)

ROY: *Comrades*, right Martin?

MARTIN: This man, Joe, is a Saint of the Right.

JOE: I know, Mr. Heller, I . . .

ROY: And you see what I mean, Martin? He's special, right?

MARTIN: Don't embarrass him, Roy.

ROY: Gravity, decency, smarts! His strength is as the strength of ten because his heart is pure! *And* he's a Royboy, one hundred percent.

MARTIN: We're on the move, Joe. On the move.

JOE: Mr. Heller, I . . .

MARTIN *(Ending backrub)*: We can't wait any longer for an answer.

(Little pause.)

JOE: Oh. Um, I . . .

ROY: Joe's a married man, Martin.

MARTIN: Aha.

ROY: With a wife. She doesn't care to go to D.C., and so Joe cannot go. And keeps us dangling. We've seen that kind of thing before, haven't we? These men and their wives.

MARTIN: Oh yes. Beware.

JOE: I really can't discuss this under . . .

MARTIN: Then *don't* discuss. Say yes, Joe.

ROY: Now.

MARTIN: Say yes I will.

ROY: Now.

Now. I'll hold my breath till you do, I'm turning blue waiting. . . . *Now*, goddammit!

MARTIN: Roy, calm down, it's not . . .

ROY: Aw, fuck it. *(He takes a letter from his jacket pocket, hands it to Joe)*

Read. Came today.

(Joe reads the first paragraph, then looks up.)

JOE: Roy. This is . . . Roy, this is terrible.

ROY: You're telling me.

A letter from the New York State Bar Association, Martin.

They're gonna try and disbar me.

MARTIN: Oh my.

JOE: Why?

ROY: Why, Martin?

MARTIN: Revenge.

ROY: The whole Establishment. Their little rules. Because I know no rules. Because I don't see the Law as a dead and arbitrary collection of antiquated dictums, thou shall, thou shalt not, because, because I know the Law's a pliable, breathing, sweating . . . *organ*, because, because . . .

MARTIN: Because he borrowed half a million from one of his clients.

ROY: Yeah, well, there's that.

MARTIN: *And* he forgot to *return* it.

JOE: Roy, that's. . . . You borrowed money from a client?

ROY: I'm deeply ashamed.

(Little pause.)

JOE *(Very sympathetic)*: Roy, you know how much I admire you. Well I mean I know you have unorthodox ways, but I'm sure you only did what you thought at the time you needed to do. And I have faith that . . .

ROY: Not so damp, please. I'll deny it was a loan. She's got no paperwork. Can't prove a fucking thing.

(Little pause. Martin studies the menu.)

JOE *(Handing back the letter, more official in tone)*: Roy I really appreciate your telling me this, and I'll do whatever I can to help.

ROY *(Holding up a hand, then, carefully)*: I'll tell you what you can do.

I'm about to be tried, Joe, by a jury that is not a jury of my peers. The disbarment committee: genteel gentleman

Brahmin lawyers, country-club men. I offend them, to these men . . . I'm what, Martin, some sort of filthy little Jewish troll?

MARTIN: Oh well, I wouldn't go so far as . . .

ROY: Oh well I would.

Very fancy lawyers, these disbarment committee lawyers, fancy lawyers with fancy corporate clients and complicated cases. Antitrust suits. Deregulation. Environmental control. Complex cases like these need Justice Department cooperation like flowers need the sun. Wouldn't you say that's an accurate assessment, Martin?

MARTIN: I'm not here, Roy. I'm not hearing any of this.

ROY: No. Of course not.

Without the light of the sun, Joe, these cases, and the fancy lawyers who represent them, will wither and die.

A well-placed friend, someone in the Justice Department, say, can turn off the sun. Cast a deep shadow on my behalf. Make them shiver in the cold. If they overstep. They would fear that.

(Pause.)

JOE: Roy. I don't understand.

ROY: You do.

(Pause.)

JOE: You're not asking me to . . .

ROY: Sssshhhh. Careful.

JOE *(A beat, then)*: Even if I said yes to the job, it would be illegal to interfere. With the hearings. It's unethical. No. I can't.

ROY: Un-ethical.

> Would you excuse us, Martin?

MARTIN: Excuse you?

ROY: Take a walk, Martin. For real.

(Martin leaves.)

ROY: Un-ethical. Are you trying to embarrass me in front of my friend?

JOE: Well it is unethical, I can't . . .

ROY: Boy, you are really something. What the fuck do you think this is, Sunday School?

JOE: No, but Roy this is . . .

ROY: This is . . . this is gastric juices churning, this is enzymes and acids, this is intestinal is what this is, bowel movement and blood-red meat—this stinks, this is *politics*, Joe, the game of being alive. And you think you're. . . . What? Above that? Above alive is what? Dead! In the clouds! You're on earth, goddammit! Plant a foot, stay a while.

> I'm sick. They smell I'm weak. They want blood this time. I must have eyes in Justice. In Justice you will protect me.

JOE: Why can't Mr. Heller . . .

ROY: Grow up, Joe. The administration can't get involved.

JOE: But I'd be part of the administration. The same as him.

ROY: Not the same. Martin's Ed's man. And Ed's Reagan's man. So Martin's Reagan's man.

> And you're mine.
> *(Little pause. He holds up the letter)*
> This will never be. Understand me?
> *(He tears the letter up)*
> I'm gonna be a lawyer, Joe, I'm gonna be a lawyer,

Joe, I'm gonna be a goddam motherfucking legally li-
censed member of the bar lawyer, just like my daddy was,
till my last bitter day on earth, Joseph, until the day
I die.

(Martin returns.)

ROY: Ah, Martin's back.
MARTIN: So are we agreed?
ROY: Joe?

(Little pause.)

JOE: I will think about it.
    (To Roy) I will.
ROY: Huh.
MARTIN: It's the fear of what comes after the doing that makes
the doing hard to do.
ROY: Amen.
MARTIN: But you can almost always live with the conse-
quences.

Scene 7

*That afternoon. On the granite steps outside the Hall of
Justice, Brooklyn. It is cold and sunny. A Sabrett wagon is
selling hot dogs. Louis, in a shabby overcoat, is sitting on the
steps contemplatively eating one. Joe enters with three hot
dogs and a can of Coke.*

JOE: Can I . . . ?

LOUIS: Oh sure. Sure. Crazy cold sun.

JOE *(Sitting)*: Have to make the best of it.
How's your friend?

LOUIS: My . . . ? Oh. He's worse. My friend is worse.

JOE: I'm sorry.

LOUIS: Yeah, well. Thanks for asking. It's nice. You're nice. I can't believe you voted for Reagan.

JOE: I hope he gets better.

LOUIS: Reagan?

JOE: Your friend.

LOUIS: He won't. Neither will Reagan.

JOE: Let's not talk politics, OK?

LOUIS *(Pointing to Joe's lunch)*: You're eating *three* of those?

JOE: Well . . . I'm . . . hungry.

LOUIS: They're really terrible for you. Full of rat-poo and beetle legs and wood shavings 'n' shit.

JOE: Huh.

LOUIS: And . . . um . . . irridium, I think. Something toxic.

JOE: You're eating one.

LOUIS: Yeah, well, the shape, I can't help myself, plus I'm *trying* to commit suicide, what's your excuse?

JOE: I don't have an excuse. I just have Pepto-Bismol.

(Joe takes a bottle of Pepto-Bismol and chugs it. Louis shudders audibly.)

JOE: Yeah I know but then I wash it down with Coke.

(He does this. Louis mimes barfing in Joe's lap. Joe pushes Louis's head away.)

JOE: Are you *always* like this?

LOUIS: I've been worrying a lot about his kids.

JOE: Whose?

LOUIS: Reagan's. Maureen and Mike and little orphan Patti and Miss Ron Reagan Jr., the you-should-pardon-the-expression heterosexual.

JOE: Ron Reagan Jr. is *not*. . . . You shouldn't just make these assumptions about people. How do you know? About him? What he is? You don't know.

LOUIS *(Doing Tallulah)*: Well darling he never sucked *my* cock but . . .

JOE: Look, if you're going to get vulgar . . .

LOUIS: No no really I mean. . . . What's it like to be the child of the Zeitgeist? To have the American Animus as your dad? It's not really a *family*, the Reagans, I read *People*, there aren't any connections there, no love, they don't ever even speak to each other except through their agents. So what's it like to be Reagan's kid? Enquiring minds want to know.

JOE: You can't believe everything you . . .

LOUIS *(Looking away)*: But . . . I think we all know what that's like. Nowadays. No connections. No responsibilities. All of us . . . falling through the cracks that separate what we owe to our selves and . . . and what we owe to love.

JOE: You just. . . . Whatever you feel like saying or doing, you don't care, you just . . . do it.

LOUIS: Do what?

JOE: It. Whatever. Whatever it is you want to do.

LOUIS: Are you trying to tell me something?

(Little pause, sexual. They stare at each other. Joe looks away.)

JOE: No, I'm just observing that you . . .

LOUIS: Impulsive.

JOE: Yes, I mean it must be scary, you . . .

LOUIS *(Shrugs)*: Land of the free. Home of the brave. Call me irresponsible.

JOE: It's kind of terrifying.

LOUIS: Yeah, well, freedom is. Heartless, too.

JOE: Oh you're not heartless.

LOUIS: You don't know.

Finish your weenie.

(He pats Joe on the knee, starts to leave.)

JOE: Um . . .

(Louis turns, looks at him. Joe searches for something to say.)

JOE: Yesterday was Sunday but I've been a little unfocused recently and I thought it was Monday. So I came here like I was going to work. And the whole place was empty. And at first I couldn't figure out why, and I had this moment of incredible . . . fear and also. . . . It just flashed through my mind: The whole Hall of Justice, it's empty, it's deserted, it's gone out of business. Forever. The people that make it run have up and abandoned it.

LOUIS *(Looking at the building)*: Creepy.

JOE: Well yes but. I felt that I was going to scream. Not because it was creepy, but because the emptiness felt so *fast*.

And . . . well, good. A . . . happy scream.

I just wondered what a thing it would be . . . if overnight everything you owe anything to, justice, or love, had really gone away. Free.

It would be . . . heartless terror. Yes. Terrible, and . . . Very great. To shed your skin, every old skin, one by one and then walk away, unencumbered, into the morning.

(*Little pause. He looks at the building*)

I can't go in there today.

LOUIS: Then don't.

JOE (*Not really hearing Louis*): I can't go in, I need . . .

(*He looks for what he needs. He takes a swig of Pepto-Bismol*)

I can't *be* this anymore. I need . . . a change, I should just . . .

LOUIS (*Not a come-on, necessarily; he doesn't want to be alone*): Want some company? For whatever?

(*Pause. Joe looks at Louis and looks away, afraid. Louis shrugs.*)

LOUIS: Sometimes, even if it scares you to death, you have to be willing to break the law. Know what I mean?

(*Another little pause.*)

JOE: Yes.

(*Another little pause.*)

LOUIS: I moved out. I moved out on my . . .

I haven't been sleeping well.

JOE: Me neither.

(*Louis goes up to Joe, licks his napkin and dabs at Joe's mouth.*)

LOUIS: Antacid moustache.

(Points to the building) Maybe the court won't con-
vene. Ever again. Maybe we are free. To do whatever.

Children of the new morning, criminal minds. Selfish
and greedy and loveless and blind. Reagan's children.

You're scared. So am I. Everybody is in the land of the
free. God help us all.

Scene 8

*Late that night. Joe at a payphone phoning Hannah at home
in Salt Lake City.*

JOE: Mom?

HANNAH: Joe?

JOE: Hi.

HANNAH: You're calling from the street. It's . . . it must be four
in the morning. What's happened?

JOE: Nothing, nothing, I . . .

HANNAH: It's Harper. Is Harper. . . . Joe? Joe?

JOE: Yeah, hi. No, Harper's fine. Well, no, she's . . . not fine.
How are you, Mom?

HANNAH: What's happened?

JOE: I just wanted to talk to you. I, uh, wanted to try something
out on you.

HANNAH: Joe, you haven't . . . have you been drinking, Joe?

JOE: Yes ma'am. I'm drunk.

HANNAH: That isn't like you.

JOE: No. I mean, who's to say?

HANNAH: Why are you out on the street at four AM? In that
crazy city. It's dangerous.

JOE: Actually, Mom, I'm not on the street. I'm near the boat-
house in the park.

HANNAH: What park?

JOE: Central Park.

HANNAH: CENTRAL PARK! Oh my Lord. What on earth
are you doing in Central Park at this time of night? Are
you . . .

Joe, I think you ought to go home right now. Call me
from home.

(Little pause)
Joe?

JOE: I come here to watch, Mom. Sometimes. Just to watch.

HANNAH: Watch what? What's there to watch at four in
the . . .

JOE: Mom, did Dad love me?

HANNAH: What?

JOE: Did he?

HANNAH: You ought to go home and call from there.

JOE: Answer.

HANNAH: Oh now really. This is maudlin. I don't like this
conversation.

JOE: Yeah, well, it gets worse from here on.

(Pause.)

HANNAH: Joe?

JOE: Mom. Momma. I'm a homosexual, Momma.
Boy, did that come out awkward.
(Pause)
Hello? Hello?
I'm a homosexual.
(Pause)
Please, Momma. Say something.

HANNAH: You're old enough to understand that your father didn't love you without being ridiculous about it.

JOE: What?

HANNAH: You're ridiculous. You're being ridiculous.

JOE: I'm . . .

What?

HANNAH: You really ought to go home now to your wife. I need to go to bed. This phone call. . . . We will just forget this phone call.

JOE: Mom.

HANNAH: No more talk. Tonight. This . . .

(Suddenly very angry) Drinking is a sin! A sin! I raised you better than that. *(She hangs up)*

Scene 9

The following morning, early. Split scene: Harper and Joe at home; Louis and Prior in Prior's hospital room. Joe and Louis have just entered. This should be fast and obviously furious; overlapping is fine; the proceedings may be a little confusing but not the final results.

HARPER: Oh God. Home. The moment of truth has arrived.

JOE: Harper.

LOUIS: I'm going to move out.

PRIOR: The fuck you are.

JOE: Harper. Please listen. I still love you very much. You're still my best buddy; I'm not going to leave you.

HARPER: No, I don't like the sound of this. I'm leaving.

LOUIS: I'm leaving.

I already have.

JOE: Please listen. Stay. This is really hard. We have to talk.

HARPER: We are talking. Aren't we. Now please shut up. OK?

PRIOR: Bastard. Sneaking off while I'm flat out here, that's low. If I could get up now I'd beat the holy shit out of you.

JOE: Did you take pills? How many?

HARPER: No pills. Bad for the . . . *(Pats stomach)*

JOE: You aren't pregnant. I called your gynecologist.

HARPER: I'm seeing a new gynecologist.

PRIOR: You have no right to do this.

LOUIS: Oh, that's ridiculous.

PRIOR: No right. It's criminal.

JOE: Forget about that. Just listen. You want the truth. This is the truth.

I knew this when I married you. I've known this I guess for as long as I've known anything, but . . . I don't know, I thought maybe that with enough effort and will I could change myself . . . but I can't . . .

PRIOR: Criminal.

LOUIS: There oughta be a law.

PRIOR: There is a law. You'll see.

JOE: I'm losing ground here, I go walking, you want to know where I walk, I . . . go to the park, or up and down 53rd Street, or places where. . . . And I keep swearing I won't go walking again, but I just can't.

LOUIS: I need some privacy.

PRIOR: That's new.

LOUIS: Everything's new, Prior.

JOE: I try to tighten my heart into a knot, a snarl, I try to learn to live dead, just numb, but then I see someone I want, and it's like a nail, like a hot spike right through my chest, and I know I'm losing.

PRIOR: Apartment too small for three? Louis and Prior comfy
but not Louis and Prior and Prior's disease?

LOUIS: Something like that.

I won't be judged by you. This isn't a crime, just—the
inevitable consequence of people who run out of—whose
limitations . . .

PRIOR: Bang bang bang. The court will come to order.

LOUIS: I mean let's talk practicalities, schedules; I'll come over
if you want, spend nights with you when I can, I can . . .

PRIOR: Has the jury reached a verdict?

LOUIS: I'm doing the best I can.

PRIOR: Pathetic. Who cares?

JOE: My whole life has conspired to bring me to this place, and I
can't despise my whole life. I think I believed when I met
you I could save you, you at least if not myself, but . . .

I don't have any sexual feelings for you, Harper. And I
don't think I ever did.

(Little pause.)

HARPER: I think you should go.

JOE: Where?

HARPER: Washington. Doesn't matter.

JOE: What are you talking about?

HARPER: Without me.

Without me, Joe. Isn't that what you want to hear?

(Little pause.)

JOE: Yes.

LOUIS: You can love someone and fail them. You can love
someone and not be able to . . .

PRIOR: You *can*, theoretically, yes. A person can, maybe an editorial "you" can love, Louis, but not *you*, specifically you, I don't know, I think you are excluded from that general category.

HARPER: You were going to save me, but the whole time you were spinning a lie. I just don't understand that.

PRIOR: A person could theoretically love and maybe many do but we both know now you can't.

LOUIS: I do.

PRIOR: You can't even say it.

LOUIS: I love you, Prior.

PRIOR: I repeat. Who cares?

HARPER: This is so scary, I want this to stop, to go back . . .

PRIOR: We have reached a verdict, your honor. This man's heart is deficient. He loves, but his love is worth nothing.

JOE: Harper . . .

HARPER: Mr. Lies, I want to get away from here. Far away. Right now. Before he starts talking again. Please, please . . .

JOE: As long as I've known you Harper you've been afraid of . . . of men hiding under the bed, men hiding under the sofa, men with knives.

PRIOR (*Shattered; almost pleading; trying to reach him*): I'm dying! You stupid fuck! Do you know what that is! Love! Do you know what love means? We lived together four-and-a-half years, you animal, you idiot.

LOUIS: I have to find some way to save myself.

JOE: Who are these men? I never understood it. Now I know.

HARPER: What?

JOE: It's me.

HARPER: It is?

PRIOR: GET OUT OF MY ROOM!

JOE: I'm the man with the knives.

HARPER: You are?

PRIOR: If I could get up now I'd kill you. I would. Go away. Go away or I'll scream.

HARPER: Oh God . . .

JOE: I'm sorry . . .

HARPER: It is you.

LOUIS: Please don't scream.

PRIOR: Go.

HARPER: I recognize you now.

LOUIS: Please . . .

JOE: Oh. Wait, I. . . . Oh!

(He covers his mouth with his hand, gags, and removes his hand, red with blood)

I'm bleeding.

(Prior screams.)

HARPER: Mr. Lies.

MR. LIES (Appearing, dressed in antarctic explorer's apparel): Right here.

HARPER: I want to go away. I can't see him anymore.

MR. LIES: Where?

HARPER: Anywhere. Far away.

MR. LIES: Absolutamento.

(Harper and Mr. Lies vanish. Joe looks up, sees that she's gone.)

PRIOR (Closing his eyes): When I open my eyes you'll be gone.

(Louis leaves.)

JOE: Harper?

PRIOR (Opening his eyes): Huh. It worked.

JOE *(Calling)*: Harper?

PRIOR: I hurt all over. I wish I was dead.

Scene 10

The same day, sunset. Hannah and Sister Ella Chapter, a real-estate saleswoman, Hannah Pitt's closest friend, in front of Hannah's house in Salt Lake City.

SISTER ELLA CHAPTER: Look at that view! A view of heaven. Like the living city of heaven, isn't it, it just fairly glimmers in the sun.

HANNAH: Glimmers.

SISTER ELLA CHAPTER: Even the stone and brick it just glimmers and glitters like heaven in the sunshine. Such a nice view you get, perched up on a canyon rim. Some kind of beautiful place.

HANNAH: It's just Salt Lake, and you're selling the house *for* me, not *to* me.

SISTER ELLA CHAPTER: I like to work up an enthusiasm for my properties.

HANNAH: Just get me a good price.

SISTER ELLA CHAPTER: Well, the market's off.

HANNAH: At least fifty.

SISTER ELLA CHAPTER: Forty'd be more like it.

HANNAH: Fifty.

SISTER ELLA CHAPTER: Wish you'd wait a bit.

HANNAH: Well I can't.

SISTER ELLA CHAPTER: Wish you would. You're about the only friend I got.

HANNAH: Oh well now.

SISTER ELLA CHAPTER: Know why I decided to like you? I decided to like you 'cause you're the only unfriendly Mormon I ever met.

HANNAH: Your wig is crooked.

SISTER ELLA CHAPTER: Fix it.

(Hannah straightens Sister Ella's wig.)

SISTER ELLA CHAPTER: New York City. All they got there is tiny rooms.

I always thought: People ought to stay put. That's why I got my license to sell real estate. It's a way of saying: Have a house! Stay put! It's a way of saying traveling's no good. Plus I needed the cash. *(She takes a pack of cigarettes out of her purse, lights one, offers pack to Hannah)*

HANNAH: Not out here, anyone could come by.

There's been days I've stood at this ledge and thought about stepping over.

It's a hard place, Salt Lake: baked dry. Abundant energy; not much intelligence. That's a combination that can wear a body out. No harm looking someplace else. I don't need much room.

My sister-in-law Libby thinks there's radon gas in the basement.

SISTER ELLA CHAPTER: Is there gas in the . . .

HANNAH: Of course not. Libby's a fool.

SISTER ELLA CHAPTER: 'Cause I'd have to include that in the description.

HANNAH: There's no gas, Ella. *(Little pause)* Give a puff. *(She takes a furtive drag of Ella's cigarette)* Put it away now.

SISTER ELLA CHAPTER: So I guess it's goodbye.

HANNAH: You'll be all right, Ella, I wasn't ever much of a friend.

SISTER ELLA CHAPTER: I'll say something but don't laugh, OK? This is the home of saints, the godliest place on earth, they say, and I think they're right. That mean there's no evil here? No. Evil's everywhere. Sin's everywhere. But this . . . is the spring of sweet water in the desert, the desert flower. Every step a Believer takes away from here is a step fraught with peril. I fear for you, Hannah Pitt, because you are my friend. Stay put. This is the right home of saints.

HANNAH: Latter-day saints.

SISTER ELLA CHAPTER: Only kind left.

HANNAH: But still. Late in the day . . . for saints and everyone. That's all. That's all.

Fifty thousand dollars for the house, Sister Ella Chapter; don't undersell. It's an impressive view.

ACT THREE:

Not-Yet-Conscious, Forward Dawning

January 1986

Scene 1

Late night, three days after the end of Act Two. The stage is completely dark. Prior is in bed in his apartment, having a nightmare. He wakes up, sits up and switches on a nightlight. He looks at his clock. Seated by the table near the bed is a man dressed in the clothing of a 13th-century British squire.

PRIOR *(Terrified)*: Who are you?
PRIOR 1: My name is Prior Walter.

(Pause.)

PRIOR: My name is Prior Walter.
PRIOR 1: I know that.
PRIOR: Explain.

PRIOR 1: You're alive. I'm not. We have the same name. What do you want me to explain?

PRIOR: A ghost?

PRIOR 1: An ancestor.

PRIOR: Not *the* Prior Walter? The Bayeux tapestry Prior Walter?

PRIOR 1: His great-great grandson. The fifth of the name.

PRIOR: I'm the thirty-fourth, I think.

PRIOR 1: Actually the thirty-second.

PRIOR: Not according to Mother.

PRIOR 1: She's including the two bastards, then; I say leave them out. I say no room for bastards. The little things you swallow . . .

PRIOR: Pills.

PRIOR 1: Pills. For the pestilence. I too . . .

PRIOR: Pestilence. . . . You too what?

PRIOR 1: The pestilence in my time was much worse than now. Whole villages of empty houses. You could look outdoors and see Death walking in the morning, dew dampening the ragged hem of his black robe. Plain as I see you now.

PRIOR: You died of the plague.

PRIOR 1: The spotty monster. Like you, alone.

PRIOR: I'm not alone.

PRIOR 1: You have no wife, no children.

PRIOR: I'm gay.

PRIOR 1: So? Be gay, dance in your altogether for all I care, what's that to do with not having children?

PRIOR: Gay homosexual, not bonny, blithe and . . . never mind.

PRIOR 1: I had twelve. When I died.

(The second ghost appears, this one dressed in the clothing of an elegant 17th-century Londoner.)

PRIOR 1 *(Pointing to Prior 2)*: And I was three years younger than him.

(Prior sees the new ghost, screams.)

PRIOR: Oh God another one.

PRIOR 2: Prior Walter. Prior to you by some seventeen others.

PRIOR 1: He's counting the bastards.

PRIOR: Are we having a convention?

PRIOR 2: We've been sent to declare her fabulous incipience. They love a well-paved entrance with lots of heralds, and . . .

PRIOR 1: The messenger come. Prepare the way. The infinite descent, a breath in air . . .

PRIOR 2: They chose us, I suspect, because of the mortal affinities. In a family as long-descended as the Walters there are bound to be a few carried off by plague.

PRIOR 1: The spotty monster.

PRIOR 2: Black Jack. Came from a water pump, half the city of London, can you imagine? His came from fleas. Yours, I understand, is the lamentable consequence of venery . . .

PRIOR 1: Fleas on rats, but who knew that?

PRIOR: Am I going to die?

PRIOR 2: We aren't allowed to discuss . . .

PRIOR 1: When you do, you don't get ancestors to help you through it. You may be surrounded by children but you die alone.

PRIOR: I'm afraid.

PRIOR 1: You should be. There aren't even torches, and the path's rocky, dark and steep.

PRIOR 2: Don't alarm him. There's good news before there's bad.

93

We two come to strew rose petal and palm leaf before the triumphal procession. Prophet. Seer. Revelator. It's a great honor for the family.

PRIOR 1: He hasn't got a family.

PRIOR 2: I meant for the Walters, for the family in the larger sense.

PRIOR *(Singing)*:

> All I want is a room somewhere,
> Far away from the cold night air . . .

PRIOR 2 *(Putting a hand on Prior's forehead)*: Calm, calm, this is no brain fever . . .

(Prior calms down, but keeps his eyes closed. The lights begin to change. Distant Glorious Music.)

PRIOR 1 *(Low chant)*:

> Adonai, Adonai,
> Olam ha-yichud,
> Zefirot, Zazahot,
> Ha-adam, ha-gadol
> Daughter of Light,
> Daughter of Splendors,
> Fluor! Phosphor!
> Lumen! Candle!

PRIOR 2 *(Simultaneously)*:

> Even now,
> From the mirror-bright halls of heaven,
> Across the cold and lifeless infinity of space,
> The Messenger comes
> Trailing orbs of light,
> Fabulous, incipient,
> Oh Prophet,
> To you . . .

PRIOR 1 and PRIOR 2:
>   Prepare, prepare,
>   The Infinite Descent,
>   A breath, a feather,
>   Glory to . . .

(They vanish.)

Scene 2

The next day. Split scene: Louis and Belize in a coffee shop. Prior is at the outpatient clinic at the hospital with Emily, the nurse; she has him on a pentamidine IV drip.

LOUIS: Why has democracy succeeded in America? Of course by succeeded I mean comparatively, not literally, not in the present, but what makes for the prospect of some sort of radical democracy spreading outward and growing up? Why does the power that was once so carefully preserved at the top of the pyramid by the original framers of the Constitution seem drawn inexorably downward and outward in spite of the best effort of the Right to stop this? I mean it's the really hard thing about being Left in this country, the American Left can't help but trip over all these petrified little fetishes: freedom, that's the worst; you know, *Jeane Kirkpatrick* for God's sake will go on and on about freedom and so what does that mean, the word freedom, when she talks about it, or human rights; you have Bush talking about human rights, and so what are these people talking about, they might as well be talking about the mating habits of Venusians, these people don't begin to know what, ontologically, freedom is or human rights, like they see these bourgeois property-based Rights-of-Man-type rights but that's not enfranchisement, not democracy, not what's implicit, what's potential within the idea, not the idea with blood in it. That's just liberalism, the worst kind of liberalism, really, bourgeois tolerance, and what I think is that what AIDS shows us is the limits of tolerance, that it's not enough to be tolerated, because when the shit hits the fan you find out how much tolerance is worth. Nothing. And underneath all the tolerance is intense, passionate hatred.

BELIZE: Uh huh.

LOUIS: Well don't you think that's true?

BELIZE: Uh huh. It is.

LOUIS: *Power* is the object, not being tolerated. Fuck assimilation. But I mean in spite of all this the thing about America, I think, is that ultimately we're different from every other nation on earth, in that, with people here of every race, we can't. . . . Ultimately what defines us isn't race, but politics. Not like any European country where there's an insurmountable fact of a kind of racial, or ethnic, monopoly, or monolith, like all Dutchmen, I mean Dutch people, are well, Dutch, and the Jews of Europe were never Europeans, just a small problem. Facing the monolith. But here there are so many small problems, it's really just a collection of small problems, the monolith is missing. Oh, I mean, of course I suppose there's the monolith of White America. White Straight Male America.

BELIZE: Which is not unimpressive, even among monoliths.

LOUIS: Well, no, but when the race thing gets taken care of, and I don't mean to minimalize how major it is, I mean I know it is, this is a really, really incredibly racist country but it's like, well, the British. I mean, all these blue-eyed pink people. And it's just weird, you know, I mean I'm not all that Jewish-looking, or . . . well, maybe I am but, you know, in New York, everyone is . . . well, not everyone, but so many are but so but in England, in London I walk into bars and I feel like Sid the Yid, you know I mean like Woody Allen in *Annie Hall*, with the payess and the gabardine coat, like never, never anywhere so much—I mean, not actively despised, not like they're Germans, who I think are still terribly anti-Semitic, and racist too, I mean black-racist,they pretend otherwise but, anyway, in London, there's just . . . and at one point I met this black gay guy from Jamaica who talked with a lilt but he said his family'd been living in London since before the Civil War—the American one—and how the English never let him forget for a minute that he wasn't blue-eyed and pink and I said yeah, me too, these people are anti-Semites and he said yeah but the British Jews have the clothing business all sewed up and blacks there can't get a foothold. And it was an incredibly awkward moment of just. . . . I mean here we were, in this bar that was gay but it was a *pub*, you know, the beams and the plaster and those horrible little, like, two-day-old fish and egg sandwiches—and just so British, so *old*, and I felt, well, there's no way out of this because both of us are, right now, too much immersed in this history, hope is dissolved in the sheer age of this place, where race is what counts and there's no real hope of change—it's the racial destiny of the Brits that matters to them, not their political destiny, whereas in America . . .

BELIZE: Here in America race doesn't count.

LOUIS: No, no, that's not. . . . I mean you *can't* be hearing that . . .

BELIZE: I . . .

LOUIS: It's—look, race, yes, but ultimately race here is a political question, right? Racists just try to use race here as a tool in a political struggle. It's not really about race. Like the spiritualists try to use that stuff, are you enlightened, are you centered, channeled, whatever, this reaching out for a spiritual past in a country where no indigenous spirits exist—only the Indians, I mean Native American spirits and we killed them off so now, there are no gods here, no ghosts and spirits in America, there are no angels in America, no spiritual past, no racial past, there's only the political, and the decoys and the ploys to maneuver around the inescapable battle of politics, the shifting downwards and outwards of political power to the people . . .

BELIZE: POWER to the People! AMEN! *(Looking at his watch) OH MY GOODNESS!* Will you look at the time, I gotta . . .

LOUIS: Do you. . . . You think this is, what, racist or naive or something?

BELIZE: Well it's certainly *something.* Look, I just remembered I have an appointment . . .

LOUIS: What? I mean I really don't want to, like, speak from some position of privilege and . . .

BELIZE: I'm sitting here, thinking, eventually he's *got* to run out of steam, so I let you rattle on and on saying about maybe seven or eight things I find really offensive.

LOUIS: What?

BELIZE: But I know you, Louis, and I know the guilt fueling this peculiar tirade is obviously already swollen bigger than your hemorrhoids.

LOUIS: I don't have hemorrhoids.

BELIZE: I hear different. May I finish?

LOUIS: Yes, but I don't have hemorrhoids.

BELIZE: So finally, when I . . .

LOUIS: Prior told you, he's an asshole, he shouldn't have . . .

BELIZE: You promised, Louis. Prior is not a subject.

LOUIS: You brought him up.

BELIZE: I brought up hemorrhoids.

LOUIS: So it's indirect. Passive-aggressive.

BELIZE: Unlike, I suppose, banging me over the head with your theory that America doesn't have a race problem.

LOUIS: Oh be fair I never said that.

BELIZE: Not exactly, but . . .

LOUIS: I said . . .

BELIZE: . . . but it was close enough, because if it'd been that blunt I'd've just walked out and . . .

LOUIS: You deliberately misinterpreted! I . . .

BELIZE: Stop interrupting! I haven't been able to . . .

LOUIS: Just let me . . .

BELIZE: NO! What, *talk*? You've been running your mouth non-stop since I got here, yaddadda yaddadda blah blah blah, up the hill, down the hill, playing with your MONOLITH . . .

LOUIS *(Overlapping)*: Well, you could have joined in at any time instead of . . .

BELIZE *(Continuing over Louis)*: . . . and girlfriend it is truly an *awesome* spectacle but I got better things to do with my time than sit here listening to this racist bullshit just because I feel sorry for you that . . .

LOUIS: I am not a racist!

BELIZE: Oh come on . . .

LOUIS: So maybe I am a racist but . . .

BELIZE: Oh I really hate that! It's no fun picking on you Louis; you're so guilty, it's like throwing darts at a glob of jello, there's no satisfying hits, just quivering, the darts just blop in and vanish.

LOUIS: I just think when you are discussing lines of oppression it gets very complicated and . . .

BELIZE: Oh is that a fact? You know, we black drag queens have a rather intimate knowledge of the complexity of the lines of . . .

LOUIS: *Ex*-black drag queen.

BELIZE: Actually ex-ex.

LOUIS: You're doing drag again?

BELIZE: I don't. . . . Maybe. I don't have to tell you. Maybe.

LOUIS: I think it's sexist.

BELIZE: I didn't ask you.

LOUIS: Well it is. The gay community, I think, has to adopt the same attitude towards drag as black women have to take towards black women blues singers.

BELIZE: Oh my we *are* walking dangerous tonight.

LOUIS: Well, it's all internalized oppression, right, I mean the masochism, the stereotypes, the . . .

BELIZE: Louis, are you deliberately trying to make me hate you?

LOUIS: No, I . . .

BELIZE: I mean, are you deliberately transforming yourself into an arrogant, sexual-political Stalinist-slash-racist flag-waving thug for my benefit?

(Pause.)

LOUIS: You know what I think?

BELIZE: What?

LOUIS: You hate me because I'm a Jew.

BELIZE: I'm leaving.

LOUIS: It's true.

BELIZE: You have no basis except your . . .

Louis, it's good to know you haven't changed; you are

still an honorary citizen of the Twilight Zone, and after your pale, pale white polemics on behalf of racial insensitivity you have a flaming *fuck* of a lot of nerve calling me an anti-Semite. Now I really gotta go.

LOUIS: You called me Lou the Jew.

BELIZE: That was a joke.

LOUIS: I didn't think it was funny. It was hostile.

BELIZE: It was three years ago.

LOUIS: So?

BELIZE: You just called yourself Sid the Yid.

LOUIS: That's not the same thing.

BELIZE: Sid the Yid is different from Lou the Jew.

LOUIS: Yes.

BELIZE: Someday you'll have to explain that to me, but right now . . .

　　You hate me because you hate black people.

LOUIS: I do not. But I do think most black people are anti-Semitic.

BELIZE: "Most black people." *That's* racist, Louis, and *I* think most Jews . . .

LOUIS: Louis Farrakhan.

BELIZE: Ed Koch.

LOUIS: Jesse Jackson.

BELIZE: Jackson. Oh really, Louis, this is . . .

LOUIS: Hymietown! Hymietown!

BELIZE: Louis, you voted for Jesse Jackson. You send checks to the Rainbow Coalition.

LOUIS: I'm ambivalent. The checks bounced.

BELIZE: All your checks bounce, Louis; you're ambivalent about everything.

LOUIS: What's that supposed to mean?

BELIZE: You may be dumber than shit but I refuse to believe you can't figure it out. Try.

LOUIS: I was never ambivalent about Prior. I love him. I do. I really do.

BELIZE: Nobody said different.

LOUIS: Love and ambivalence are. . . . Real love isn't ambivalent.

BELIZE: "Real love isn't ambivalent." I'd swear that's a line from my favorite bestselling paperback novel, *In Love with the Night Mysterious*, except I don't think you ever read it.

(Pause.)

LOUIS: I never read it, no.

BELIZE: You ought to. Instead of spending the rest of your life trying to get through *Democracy in America*. It's about this white woman whose Daddy owns a plantation in the Deep South in the years before the Civil War—the American one—and her name is Margaret, and she's in love with her Daddy's number-one slave, and his name is Thaddeus, and she's married but her white slave-owner husband has AIDS: Antebellum Insufficiently Developed Sexorgans. And there's a lot of hot stuff going down when Margaret and Thaddeus can catch a spare torrid ten under the cotton-picking moon, and then of course the Yankees come, and they set the slaves free, and the slaves string up old Daddy, and so on. Historical fiction. Somewhere in there I recall Margaret and Thaddeus find the time to discuss the nature of love; her face is reflecting the flames of the burning plantation—you know, the way white people do—and his black face is dark in the night and she says to him, "Thaddeus, real love isn't ever ambivalent."

(Little pause. Emily enters and turns off IV drip.)

BELIZE: Thaddeus looks at her; he's contemplating her thesis; and he isn't sure he agrees.

EMILY *(Removing IV drip from Prior's arm)*: Treatment number . . . *(Consulting chart)* four.

PRIOR: Pharmaceutical miracle. Lazarus breathes again.

LOUIS: Is he. . . . How bad is he?

BELIZE: You want the laundry list?

EMILY: Shirt off, let's check the . . .

(Prior takes his shirt off. She examines his lesions.)

BELIZE: There's the weight problem and the shit problem and the morale problem.

EMILY: Only six. That's good. Pants.

(He drops his pants. He's naked. She examines.)

BELIZE: And. He thinks he's going crazy.

EMILY: Looking good. What else?

PRIOR: Ankles sore and swollen, but the leg's better. The nausea's mostly gone with the little orange pills. BM's pure liquid but not bloody anymore, for now, my eye doctor says everything's OK, for now, my dentist says "Yuck!" when he sees my fuzzy tongue, and now he wears little condoms on his thumb and forefinger. And a mask. So what? My dermatologist is in Hawaii and my mother . . . well leave my mother out of it. Which is usually where my mother is, out of it. My glands are like walnuts, my weight's holding steady for week two, and a friend died two days ago of bird tuberculosis; bird tuberculosis; that scared me and I didn't go to the funeral today because he was an Irish Catholic and it's probably open casket and I'm afraid of . . . something, the bird TB or seeing him or. . . . So I guess I'm doing OK. Except for of course I'm going nuts.

EMILY: We ran the toxoplasmosis series and there's no indication . . .

PRIOR: I know, I know, but I feel like something terrifying is on its way, you know, like a missile from outer space, and it's plummeting down towards the earth, and I'm ground zero, and . . . I am generally known where I am known as one cool, collected queen. And I am ruffled.

EMILY: There's really nothing to worry about. I think that shochen bamromim hamtzeh menucho nechono al kanfey haschino.

PRIOR: What?

EMILY: Everything's fine. Bemaalos k'doshim ut'horim kezohar horokeea mazhirim . . .

PRIOR: Oh I don't understand what you're . . .

EMILY: Es nishmas Prior sheholoch leolomoh, baavur shenodvoo z'dokoh b'ad hazkoras nishmosoh.

PRIOR: Why are you doing that?! Stop it! Stop it!

EMILY: Stop what?

PRIOR: You were just . . . weren't you just speaking in Hebrew or something.

EMILY: *Hebrew? (Laughs)* I'm basically Italian-American. No. I didn't speak in Hebrew.

PRIOR: Oh no, oh God please I really think I . . .

EMILY: Look, I'm sorry, I have a waiting room full of. . . . I think you're one of the lucky ones, you'll live for years, probably—you're pretty healthy for someone with no immune system. Are you seeing someone? Loneliness is a danger. A therapist?

PRIOR: No, I don't need to see anyone, I just . . .

EMILY: Well think about it. You aren't going crazy. You're just under a lot of stress. No wonder . . . *(She starts to write in his chart)*

(Suddenly there is an astonishing blaze of light, a huge chord sounded by a gigantic choir, and a great book with steel pages mounted atop a molten-red pillar pops up from the stage floor. The book opens; there is a large Aleph inscribed on its pages, which bursts into flames. Immediately the book slams shut and disappears instantly under the floor as the lights become normal again. Emily notices none of this, writing. Prior is agog.)

EMILY *(Laughing, exiting)*: Hebrew . . .

(Prior flees.)

LOUIS: Help me.
BELIZE: I beg your pardon?
LOUIS: You're a nurse, give me something, I . . . don't know what to do anymore, I. . . . Last week at work I screwed up the Xerox machine like permanently and so I . . . then I tripped on the subway steps and my glasses broke and I cut my forehead, here, see, and now I can't see much and my forehead . . . it's like the Mark of Cain, stupid, right, but it won't heal and every morning I see it and I think, Biblical things, Mark of Cain, Judas Iscariot and his silver and his noose, people who . . . in betraying what they love betray what's truest in themselves, I feel . . . nothing but cold for myself, just cold, and every night I miss him, I miss him so much but then . . . those sores, and the smell and . . . where I thought it was going. . . . I could be . . . I could be sick too, maybe I'm sick too. I don't know.

Belize. Tell him I love him. Can you do that?

BELIZE: I've thought about it for a very long time, and I still don't understand what love is. Justice is simple. Democracy is simple. Those things are unambivalent. But love is very hard. And it goes bad for you if you violate the hard law of love.

LOUIS: I'm dying.

BELIZE: He's dying. You just wish you were.

Oh cheer up, Louis. Look at that heavy sky out there.

LOUIS: Purple.

BELIZE: *Purple?* Boy, what kind of a homosexual are you, anyway? That's not purple, Mary, that color up there is *(Very grand)* mauve.

All day today it's felt like Thanksgiving. Soon, this . . . ruination will be blanketed white. You can smell it—can you smell it?

LOUIS: Smell what?

BELIZE: Softness, compliance, forgiveness, grace.

LOUIS: No . . .

BELIZE: I can't help you learn that. I can't help you, Louis. You're not my business. *(He exits)*

(Louis puts his head in his hands, inadvertently touching his cut forehead.)

LOUIS: Ow FUCK! *(He stands slowly, looks towards where Belize exited)* Smell what?

(He looks both ways to be sure no one is watching, then inhales deeply, and is surprised) Huh. Snow.

Scene 3

Same day. Harper in a very white, cold place, with a brilliant blue sky above; a delicate snowfall. She is dressed in a beautiful snowsuit. The sound of the sea, faint.

HARPER: Snow! Ice! Mountains of ice! Where am I? I . . . I feel better, I do, I . . . feel better. There are ice crystals in my lungs, wonderful and sharp. And the snow smells like cold, crushed peaches. And there's something . . . some current of blood in the wind, how strange, it has that iron taste.

MR. LIES: Ozone.

HARPER: Ozone! Wow! Where am I?

MR. LIES: The Kingdom of Ice, the bottommost part of the world.

HARPER *(Looking around, then realizing)*: Antarctica. This is Antarctica!

MR. LIES: Cold shelter for the shattered. No sorrow here, tears freeze.

HARPER: Antarctica, Antarctica, oh boy oh boy, LOOK at this, I. . . . Wow, I must've really snapped the tether, huh?

MR. LIES: Apparently . . .

HARPER: That's great. I want to stay here forever. Set up camp. Build things. Build a city, an enormous city made up of frontier forts, dark wood and green roofs and high gates made of pointed logs and bonfires burning on every street corner. I should build by a river. Where are the forests?

MR. LIES: No timber here. Too cold. Ice, no trees.

HARPER: Oh details! I'm sick of details! I'll plant them and grow them. I'll live off caribou fat, I'll melt it over the bonfires and drink it from long, curved goat-horn cups.

It'll be great. I want to make a new world here. So that I
never have to go home again.

MR. LIES: As long as it lasts. Ice has a way of melting . . .

HARPER: No. Forever. I can have anything I want here—maybe
even companionship, someone who has . . . desire for me.
You, maybe.

MR. LIES: It's against the by-laws of the International Order of
Travel Agents to get involved with clients. Rules are rules.
Anyway, I'm not the one you really want.

HARPER: There isn't anyone . . . maybe an Eskimo. Who could
ice-fish for food. And help me build a nest for when the
baby comes.

MR. LIES: There are no Eskimo in Antarctica. And you're not
really pregnant. You made that up.

HARPER: Well all of this is made up. So if the snow feels cold
I'm pregnant. Right? Here, I can be pregnant. And I can
have any kind of a baby I want.

MR. LIES: This is a retreat, a vacuum, its virtue is that it lacks
everything; deep-freeze for feelings. You can be numb
and safe here, that's what you came for. Respect the
delicate ecology of your delusions.

HARPER: You mean like no Eskimo in Antarctica.

MR. LIES: Correcto. Ice and snow, no Eskimo. Even hallucinations have laws.

HARPER: Well then who's that?

(The Eskimo appears.)

MR. LIES: An Eskimo.

HARPER: An antarctic Eskimo. A fisher of the polar deep.

MR. LIES: There's something wrong with this picture.

(The Eskimo beckons.)

HARPER: I'm going to like this place. It's my own National Geographic Special! Oh! Oh! *(She holds her stomach)* I think . . . I think I felt her kicking. Maybe I'll give birth to a baby covered with thick white fur, and that way she won't be cold. My breasts will be full of hot cocoa so she doesn't get chilly. And if it gets really cold, she'll have a pouch I can crawl into. Like a marsupial. We'll mend together. That's what we'll do; we'll mend.

Scene 4

Same day. An abandoned lot in the South Bronx. A homeless Woman is standing near an oil drum in which a fire is burning. Snowfall. Trash around. Hannah enters dragging two heavy suitcases.

HANNAH: Excuse me? I said excuse me? Can you tell me where I am? Is this Brooklyn? Do you know a Pineapple Street? Is there some sort of bus or train or . . . ?

I'm lost, I just arrived from Salt Lake. City. Utah? I took the bus that I was told to take and I got off—well it was the very last stop, so I had to get off, and I *asked* the driver was this Brooklyn, and he nodded yes but he was from one of those foreign countries where they think it's good manners to nod at everything even if you have no idea what it is you're nodding at, and in truth I think he spoke no English at all, which I think would make him ineligible for employment on public transportation. The public being English-speaking, mostly. Do you speak English?

(The Woman nods.)

HANNAH: I was supposed to be met at the airport by my son. He didn't show and I don't wait more than three and three-quarters hours for *anyone*. I should have been patient, I guess, I. . . . Is this . . .

WOMAN: Bronx.

HANNAH: Is that. . . . The *Bronx*? Well how in the name of Heaven did I get to the Bronx when the bus driver said . . .

WOMAN *(Talking to herself)*: Slurp slurp slurp will you STOP that disgusting slurping! YOU DISGUSTING SLURPING FEEDING ANIMAL! Feeding yourself, just feeding yourself, what would it matter, to you or to ANYONE, if you just stopped. Feeding. And DIED?

(Pause.)

HANNAH: Can you just tell me where I . . .

WOMAN: Why was the Kosciusko Bridge named after a Polack?

HANNAH: I don't know what you're . . .

WOMAN: That was a joke.

HANNAH: Well what's the punchline?

WOMAN: I don't know.

HANNAH *(Looking around desperately)*: Oh for pete's sake, is there anyone else who . . .

WOMAN *(Again, to herself)*: Stand further off you fat loathsome whore, you can't have any more of this soup, slurp slurp slurp you animal, and the—I know you'll just go pee it all away and where will you do that? Behind what bush? It's FUCKING COLD out here and I . . .

Oh that's right, because it was supposed to have been a tunnel!

That's not very funny.

Have you read the prophecies of Nostradamus?

HANNAH: Who?

WOMAN: Some guy I went out with once somewhere, Nostradamus. Prophet, outcast, eyes like. . . . Scary shit, he . . .

HANNAH: Shut up. Please. Now I want you to stop jabbering for a minute and pull your wits together and tell me how to get to Brooklyn. Because you know! And you are going to tell me! Because there is no one else around to tell me and I am wet and cold and I am very angry! So I am sorry you're psychotic but just make the effort—take a deep breath—DO IT!

(Hannah and the Woman breathe together.)

HANNAH: That's good. Now exhale.

(They do.)

HANNAH: Good. Now how do I get to Brooklyn?

WOMAN: Don't know. Never been. Sorry. Want some soup?

HANNAH: Manhattan? Maybe you know . . . I don't suppose you know the location of the Mormon Visitor's . . .

WOMAN: 65th and Broadway.

HANNAH: How do you . . .

WOMAN: Go there all the time. Free movies. Boring, but you can stay all day.

HANNAH: Well. . . . So how do I . . .

WOMAN: Take the D Train. Next block make a right.

HANNAH: Thank you.

WOMAN: Oh yeah. In the new century I think we will all be insane.

Scene 5

Same day. Joe and Roy in the study of Roy's brownstone. Roy is wearing an elegant bathrobe. He has made a considerable effort to look well. He isn't well, and he hasn't succeeded much in looking it.

JOE: I can't. The answer's no. I'm sorry.

ROY: Oh, well, apologies . . .

　　　I can't see that there's anyone asking for apologies.

(Pause.)

JOE: I'm sorry, Roy.

ROY: Oh, well, apologies.

JOE: My wife is missing, Roy. My mother's coming from Salt Lake to . . . to help look, I guess. I'm supposed to be at the airport now, picking her up but. . . . I just spent two days in a hospital, Roy, with a bleeding ulcer, I was spitting up blood.

ROY: Blood, huh? Look, I'm very busy here and . . .

JOE: It's just a job.

ROY: A job? A *job*? *Washington*! Dumb Utah Mormon hick shit!

JOE: Roy . . .

ROY: *WASHINGTON!* When Washington called me I was younger than you, you think I said "Aw fuck no I can't go I got two fingers up my asshole and a little moral nosebleed to boot!" When Washington calls you my pretty young punk friend you go or you can go fuck yourself sideways 'cause the train has pulled out of the station, and you are *out*, nowhere, out in the cold. Fuck you, Mary Jane, get outta here.

JOE: Just let me . . .

ROY: Explain? Ephemera. You broke my heart. Explain that.
Explain that.

JOE: I love you. Roy.

There's so much that I want, to be . . . what you see in
me, I want to be a participant in the world, in your world,
Roy, I want to be capable of that, I've tried, really I have
but . . . I can't do this. Not because I don't believe in you,
but because I believe in you so much, in what you stand
for, at heart, the order, the decency. I would give anything
to protect you, but. . . . There are laws I can't break. It's
too ingrained. It's not me. There's enough damage I've
already done.

Maybe you were right, maybe I'm dead.

ROY: You're not dead, boy, you're a sissy.

You love me; that's moving, I'm moved. It's nice to be
loved. I warned you about her, didn't I, Joe? But you don't
listen to me, why, because you say Roy is smart and Roy's
a friend but Roy . . . well, he isn't nice, and you wanna
be nice. Right? A nice, nice man!

(Little pause)

You know what my greatest accomplishment was, Joe,
in my life, what I am able to look back on and be proudest
of? And I have helped make Presidents and unmake them
and mayors and more goddam judges than anyone in
NYC ever—AND several million dollars, tax-free—and
what do you think means the most to me?

You ever hear of Ethel Rosenberg? Huh, Joe, huh?

JOE: Well, yeah, I guess I. . . . Yes.

ROY: Yes. Yes. You have heard of Ethel Rosenberg. Yes. Maybe
you even read about her in the history books.

If it wasn't for me, Joe, Ethel Rosenberg would be
alive today, writing some personal-advice column for *Ms.*

magazine. She isn't. Because during the trial, Joe, I was on the phone every day, talking with the judge . . .

JOE: Roy . . .

ROY: Every day, doing what I do best, talking on the telephone, making sure that timid Yid nebbish on the bench did his duty to America, to history. That sweet unprepossessing woman, two kids, boo-hoo-hoo, reminded us all of our little Jewish mamas—she came this close to getting life; I pleaded till I wept to put her in the chair. Me. I did that. I would have fucking pulled the switch if they'd have let me. Why? Because I fucking hate traitors. Because I fucking hate communists. Was it legal? Fuck legal. Am I a nice man? Fuck nice. They say terrible things about me in the *Nation*. Fuck the *Nation*. You want to be Nice, or you want to be Effective? Make the law, or subject to it. Choose. Your wife chose. A week from today, she'll be back. SHE knows how to get what SHE wants. Maybe I ought to send *her* to Washington.

JOE: I don't believe you.

ROY: Gospel.

JOE: You can't possibly mean what you're saying.

Roy, you were the Assistant United States Attorney on the Rosenberg case, ex-parte communication with the judge during the trial would be . . . censurable, at least, probably conspiracy and . . . in a case that resulted in execution, it's . . .

ROY: What? Murder?

JOE: You're not well is all.

ROY: What do you mean, not well? Who's not well?

(Pause.)

JOE: You said . . .

roy: No I didn't. I said what?

joe: Roy, you have cancer.

roy: No I don't.

(Pause.)

joe: You told me you were dying.

roy: What the fuck are you talking about, Joe? I never said that. I'm in perfect health. There's not a goddam thing wrong with me.
(He smiles)
Shake?

(Joe hesitates. He holds out his hand to Roy. Roy pulls Joe into a close, strong clinch.)

roy *(More to himself than to Joe)*: It's OK that you hurt me because I love you, baby Joe. That's why I'm so rough on you.

(Roy releases Joe. Joe backs away a step or two.)

roy: Prodigal son. The world will wipe its dirty hands all over you.

joe: It already has, Roy.

roy: Now go.

(Roy shoves Joe, hard. Joe turns to leave. Roy stops him, turns him around.)

roy *(Smoothing Joe's lapels, tenderly)*: I'll always be here, waiting for you . . .

(Then again, with sudden violence, he pulls Joe close, violently)

What did you want from me, what was all this, what do you want, treacherous ungrateful little . . .

(Joe, very close to belting Roy, grabs him by the front of his robe, and propels him across the length of the room. He holds Roy at arm's length, the other arm ready to hit.)

ROY *(Laughing softly, almost pleading to be hit)*: Transgress a little, Joseph.

(Joe releases Roy.)

ROY: There are so many laws; find one you can break.

(Joe hesitates, then leaves, backing out. When Joe has gone, Roy doubles over in great pain, which he's been hiding throughout the scene with Joe.)

ROY: Ah, Christ . . .
Andy! Andy! Get in here! Andy!

(The door opens, but it isn't Andy. A small Jewish Woman dressed modestly in a fifties hat and coat stands in the doorway. The room darkens.)

ROY: Who the fuck are you? The new nurse?

(The figure in the doorway says nothing. She stares at Roy. A pause. Roy looks at her carefully, gets up, crosses to her. He crosses back to the chair, sits heavily.)

ROY: Aw, fuck. Ethel.

ETHEL ROSENBERG *(Her manner is friendly, her voice is ice-cold)*: You don't look good, Roy.

ROY: Well, Ethel. I don't feel good.

ETHEL ROSENBERG: But you lost a lot of weight. That suits you. You were heavy back then. Zaftig, mit hips.

ROY: I haven't been that heavy since 1960. We were all heavier back then, before the body thing started. Now I look like a skeleton. They stare.

ETHEL ROSENBERG: The shit's really hit the fan, huh, Roy?

(Little pause. Roy nods.)

ETHEL ROSENBERG: Well the fun's just started.

ROY: What is this, Ethel, Halloween? You trying to scare me?

(Ethel says nothing.)

ROY: Well you're wasting your time! I'm scarier than you any day of the week! So beat it, Ethel! BOOO! BETTER DEAD THAN RED! Somebody trying to shake me up? HAH HAH! From the throne of God in heaven to the belly of hell, you can all fuck yourselves and then go jump in the lake because I'M NOT AFRAID OF YOU OR DEATH OR HELL OR ANYTHING!

ETHEL ROSENBERG: Be seeing you soon, Roy. Julius sends his regards.

ROY: Yeah, well send this to Julius!

(He flips the bird in her direction, stands and moves towards her. Halfway across the room he slumps to the floor, breathing laboriously, in pain.)

ETHEL ROSENBERG: You're a very sick man, Roy.

ROY: Oh God . . . ANDY!

ETHEL ROSENBERG: Hmmm. He doesn't hear you, I guess. We should call the ambulance.

> *(She goes to the phone)*
> Hah! Buttons! Such things they got now.
> What do I dial, Roy?

(Pause. Roy looks at her, then:)

ROY: 911.

ETHEL ROSENBERG *(Dials the phone)*: It sings!

> *(Imitating dial tones)* La la la . . .
> Huh.
> Yes, you should please send an ambulance to the home of Mister Roy Cohn, the famous lawyer.
> What's the address, Roy?

ROY *(A beat, then)*: 244 East 87th.

ETHEL ROSENBERG: 244 East 87th Street. No apartment number, he's got the whole building.

> My name? *(A beat)* Ethel Greenglass Rosenberg.
> *(Small smile)* Me? No I'm not related to Mr. Cohn. An old friend.
> *(She hangs up)*
> They said a minute.

ROY: I have all the time in the world.

ETHEL ROSENBERG: You're immortal.

ROY: I'm immortal. Ethel. *(He forces himself to stand)*

> I have *forced* my way into history. I ain't never gonna die.

ETHEL ROSENBERG *(A little laugh, then)*: History is about to crack wide open. Millennium approaches.

Scene 6

Late that night. Prior's bedroom. Prior 1 watching Prior in bed, who is staring back at him, terrified. Tonight Prior 1 is dressed in weird alchemical robes and hat over his historical clothing and he carries a long palm-leaf bundle.

PRIOR 1: Tonight's the night! Aren't you excited? Tonight she arrives! Right through the roof! Ha-adam, Ha-gadol . . .

PRIOR 2 *(Appearing, similarly attired)*: Lumen! Phosphor! Fluor! Candle! An unending billowing of scarlet and . . .

PRIOR: Look. Garlic. A mirror. Holy water. A crucifix. FUCK OFF! Get the fuck out of my room! GO!

PRIOR 1 *(To Prior 2)*: Hard as a hickory knob, I'll bet.

PRIOR 2: We all tumesce when they approach. We wax full, like moons.

PRIOR 1: Dance.

PRIOR: Dance?

PRIOR 1: Stand up, dammit, give us your hands, dance!

PRIOR 2: Listen . . .

(A lone oboe begins to play a little dance tune.)

PRIOR 2: Delightful sound. Care to dance?

PRIOR: Please leave me alone, please just let me sleep . . .

PRIOR 2: Ah, he wants someone familiar. A partner who knows his steps. *(To Prior)* Close your eyes. Imagine . . .

PRIOR: I don't . . .

PRIOR 2: Hush. Close your eyes.

(Prior does.)

PRIOR 2: Now open them.

(Prior does. Louis appears. He looks gorgeous. The music builds gradually into a full-blooded, romantic dance tune.)

PRIOR: Lou.

LOUIS: Dance with me.

PRIOR: I can't, my leg, it hurts at night . . .
    Are you . . . a ghost, Lou?

LOUIS: No. Just spectral. Lost to myself. Sitting all day on cold park benches. Wishing I could be with you. Dance with me, babe . . .

(Prior stands up. The leg stops hurting. They begin to dance. The music is beautiful.)

PRIOR 1 *(To Prior 2)*: Hah. Now I see why he's got no children. He's a sodomite.

PRIOR 2: Oh be quiet, you medieval gnome, and let them dance.

PRIOR 1: I'm not interfering, I've done my bit. Hooray, hooray, the messenger's come, now I'm blowing off. I don't like it here.

(Prior 1 vanishes.)

PRIOR 2: The twentieth century. Oh dear, the world has gotten so terribly, terribly old.

(Prior 2 vanishes. Louis and Prior waltz happily. Lights fade back to normal. Louis vanishes.
    Prior dances alone.
    Then suddenly, the sound of wings fills the room.)

Scene 7

Split scene: Prior alone in his apartment; Louis alone in the park.

Again, a sound of beating wings.

PRIOR: Oh don't come in here don't come in . . . LOUIS!!
   No. My name is Prior Walter, I am . . . the scion of an ancient line, I am . . . abandoned I . . . no, my name is . . . is . . . Prior and I live . . . *here and now,* and . . . in the dark, in the dark, the Recording Angel opens its hundred eyes and snaps the spine of the Book of Life and . . . hush! Hush!
   I'm talking nonsense, I . . .
   No more mad scene, hush, hush . . .

(Louis in the park on a bench. Joe approaches, stands at a distance. They stare at each other, then Louis turns away.)

LOUIS: Do you know the story of Lazarus?
JOE: Lazarus?
LOUIS: Lazarus. I can't remember what happens, exactly.
JOE: I don't. . . . Well, he was dead, Lazarus, and Jesus breathed life into him. He brought him back from death.
LOUIS: Come here often?
JOE: No. Yes. Yes.
LOUIS: Back from the dead. You believe that really happened?
JOE: I don't know anymore what I believe.
LOUIS: This is quite a coincidence. Us meeting.
JOE: I followed you.
   From work. I . . . followed you here.

(Pause.)

LOUIS: You followed me.

You probably saw me that day in the washroom and thought: there's a sweet guy, sensitive, cries for friends in trouble.

JOE: Yes.

LOUIS: You thought maybe I'll cry for you.

JOE: Yes.

LOUIS: Well I fooled you. Crocodile tears. Nothing . . . *(He touches his heart, shrugs)*

(Joe reaches tentatively to touch Louis's face.)

LOUIS *(Pulling back)*: What are you doing? Don't do that.

JOE *(Withdrawing his hand)*: Sorry. I'm sorry.

LOUIS: I'm . . . just not . . . I think, if you touch me, your hand might fall off or something. Worse things have happened to people who have touched me.

JOE: Please.

Oh, boy . . .

Can I . . .

I . . . want . . . to touch you. Can I please just touch you . . . um, here?

(He puts his hand on one side of Louis's face. He holds it there)

I'm going to hell for doing this.

LOUIS: Big deal. You think it could be any worse than New York City?

(He puts his hand on Joe's hand. He takes Joe's hand away from his face, holds it for a moment, then) Come on.

JOE: Where?

LOUIS: Home. With me.

JOE: This makes no sense. I mean I don't know you.

LOUIS: Likewise.

JOE: And what you do know about me you don't like.

LOUIS: The Republican stuff?

JOE: Yeah, well for starters.

LOUIS: I don't not like that. I *hate* that.

JOE: So why on earth should we . . .

(Louis goes to Joe and kisses him.)

LOUIS: Strange bedfellows. I don't know. I never made it with one of the damned before.

I would really rather not have to spend tonight alone.

JOE: I'm a pretty terrible person, Louis.

LOUIS: Lou.

JOE: No, I really really am. I don't think I deserve being loved.

LOUIS: There? See? We already have a lot in common.

(Louis stands, begins to walk away. He turns, looks back at Joe. Joe follows. They exit.)

(Prior listens. At first no sound, then once again, the sound of beating wings, frighteningly near.)

PRIOR: That sound, that sound, it. . . . What is that, like birds or something, like a *really* big bird, I'm frightened, I . . . no, no fear, find the anger, find the . . . anger, my blood is clean, my brain is fine, I can handle pressure, I am a gay man and I am used to pressure, to trouble, I am tough and strong and. . . . Oh. Oh my goodness. I . . . *(He is washed over by an intense sexual feeling)* Ooohhhh. . . . I'm hot,

I'm . . . so . . . aw Jeez what is going on here I . . . must
have a fever I . . .

*(The bedside lamp flickers wildly as the bed begins to roll
forward and back. There is a deep bass creaking and groaning
from the bedroom ceiling, like the timbers of a ship under
immense stress, and from above a fine rain of plaster dust.)*

PRIOR: OH!
    PLEASE, OH PLEASE! Something's coming in
here, I'm scared, I don't like this at all, something's approaching and I. . . . OH!

*(There is a great blaze of triumphal music, heralding. The
light turns an extraordinary harsh, cold, pale blue, then a rich,
brilliant warm golden color, then a hot, bilious green, and
then finally a spectacular royal purple. Then silence.)*

PRIOR *(An awestruck whisper)*: God almighty . . .
    Very Steven Spielberg.

*(A sound, like a plummeting meteor, tears down from very,
very far above the earth, hurtling at an incredible velocity
towards the bedroom; the light seems to be sucked out of the
room as the projectile approaches; as the room reaches darkness, we hear a terrifying CRASH as something immense
strikes earth; the whole building shudders and a part of the
bedroom ceiling, lots of plaster and lathe and wiring, crashes
to the floor. And then in a shower of unearthly white light,
spreading great opalescent gray-silver wings, the Angel descends into the room and floats above the bed.)*

ANGEL:

Greetings, Prophet;
The Great Work begins:
The Messenger has arrived.

(Blackout.)

END OF PART ONE

Angels in America

Part Two: PERESTROIKA

*This revised version of Perestroika
was completed September 1995*

*First draft completed at the Russian River
April 11, 1991*

The actors, directors and designers who have worked on the play transformed it. The following section is a list of those productions, and the artists who participated, during the course of which the text was being developed. There have been many other productions, some of them exceptionally beautiful, which haven't been included simply because they were mounted after the playwriting was "finished."

Perestroika was first performed as a staged reading in May 1991 by the Eureka Theatre Company in San Francisco. It was directed by David Esbjornson. Sets were designed by Tom Kamm, costumes by Sandra Woodall and lights by Jack Carpenter and Jim Cave. The cast was as follows:

THE ANGEL	*Ellen McLaughlin*
PRIOR WALTER	*Stephen Spinella*
HARPER PITT	*Anne Darragh*
JOE PITT	*Michael Scott Ryan*
HANNAH PITT	*Kathleen Chalfant*
BELIZE	*Harry Waters Jr.*
ROY COHN	*John Bellucci*
LOUIS IRONSON	*Michael Ornstein*

The play was workshopped at the Mark Taper Forum in Los Angeles in May 1992. Oskar Eustis and Tony Taccone directed the staged reading. The cast was as follows:

THE ANGEL	*Ellen McLaughlin*
PRIOR WALTER	*Stephen Spinella*
HARPER PITT	*Cynthia Mace*
JOE PITT	*Jeffrey King*
HANNAH PITT	*Kathleen Chalfant*
BELIZE	*Harry Waters Jr.*
ROY COHN	*Larry Pressman*
LOUIS IRONSON	*Joe Mantello*

The world premiere of *Perestroika* was presented by the Mark Taper Forum in November 1992, directed by Oskar Eustis and Tony Taccone, with sets designed by John Conklin, lights by Pat Collins, costumes by Gabriel Berry and music by Mel Marvin. The cast was as follows:

THE ANGEL	*Ellen McLaughlin*
PRIOR WALTER	*Stephen Spinella*
HARPER PITT	*Cynthia Mace*
JOE PITT	*Jeffrey King*
HANNAH PITT	*Kathleen Chalfant*
BELIZE	*K. Todd Freeman*
ROY COHN	*Ron Leibman*
LOUIS IRONSON	*Joe Mantello*

The play was presented by New York University/Tisch School of the Arts in April 1993. It was directed by Michael Mayer, with sets by Tony Cisek and Andrew Hall, lights by Jack Mehler, costumes by Robin J. Orloff and music by Michael Ward. The cast was as follows:

THE ANGEL	*Jenna Stern*
PRIOR WALTER	*Daniel Zelman*
HARPER PITT	*Debra Messing*
JOE PITT	*Robert Carin*

HANNAH PITT	*Vivienne Benesch*
BELIZE	*Mark Douglas*
ROY COHN	*Ben Shenkman*
LOUIS IRONSON	*Johnny Garcia*

The play opened in London on November 20, 1993, in a production at the Royal National Theatre of Great Britain, directed by Declan Donellan, designed by Nick Ormerod, with music by Paddy Cuneen and lights by Mick Hughes. The cast was as follows:

PRELAPSARIANOV/THE RABBI	*Harry Towb*
THE ANGEL	*Nancy Crane*
PRIOR WALTER	*Stephen Dillane*
HARPER PITT	*Clare Holman*
JOE PITT	*Daniel Craig*
HANNAH PITT	*Susan Engel*
BELIZE	*Joseph Mydell*
ROY COHN	*David Schofield*
LOUIS IRONSON	*Jason Isaacs*

Perestroika opened in New York at the Walter Kerr Theatre on November 23, 1993, in a production directed by George C. Wolfe with sets by Robin Wagner, lights by Jules Fisher, costumes by Toni-Leslie James and music by Anthony Davis. The cast was as follows:

THE ANGEL	*Ellen McLaughlin*
PRIOR WALTER	*Stephen Spinella*
HARPER PITT	*Marcia Gay Harden*
JOE PITT	*David Marshall Grant*
HANNAH PITT	*Kathleen Chalfant*
BELIZE	*Jeffrey Wright*

ROY COHN	*Ron Leibman*
LOUIS IRONSON	*Joe Mantello*

Perestroika was presented by the American Conservatory Theater in San Francisco in September 1994, directed by Mark Wing-Davey, with sets designed by Kate Edmunds, lights by Christopher Akerlind and costumes by Catherine Zuber. The cast was as follows:

THE ANGEL	*Lise Bruneau*
PRIOR WALTER	*Garret Dillahunt*
HARPER PITT	*Julia Gibson*
JOE PITT	*Steven Culp*
HANNAH PITT	*Cristine McMurdo-Wallis*
BELIZE	*Gregory Wallace*
ROY COHN	*Peter Zapp*
LOUIS IRONSON	*Ben Shenkman*

The national touring production of *Perestroika* began its run on September 29, 1994, at the Royal George Theatre in Chicago. It was directed by Michael Mayer, supervised by George C. Wolfe, with sets by David Gallo, lights by Brian MacDevitt, costumes by Michael Krass and music by Michael Ward. The cast was as follows:

THE ANGEL	*Carolyn Swift*
PRIOR WALTER	*Robert Sella*
HARPER PITT	*Kate Goehring*
JOE PITT	*Philip Earl Johnson*
HANNAH PITT	*Barbara Robertson*
BELIZE	*Reg Flowers*
ROY COHN	*Jonathan Hadary*
LOUIS IRONSON	*Peter Birkenhead*

Acknowledgments

I've been working on *Perestroika* since 1989. In the process I've accumulated many debts.

Abundant support, both financial and emotional, was provided by my parents, Bill and Sylvia Kushner, and my aunt Martha Deutscher. My father has been terrifically helpful as *Perestroika* has come to completion.

My brother and sister, Eric and Lesley Kushner, have supported me both in my work and in the difficult process of coming out; without their love and enthusiasm writing this would never have been possible. The same is true for Mark Bronnenberg, to whom *Millennium Approaches* was dedicated.

Dot and Jerry Edelstien, and Marcia, Tony and Alex Cunha made homes away from home for me.

Jim Nicola of New York Theatre Workshop has encouraged and advised me all the way, and so has Rosemarie Tichler of the New York Shakespeare Festival. Together they shed blood for the play, literally; they have won my purple heart.

Joyce Ketay, the Wonder-Agent, and her associate Carl Mulert, have been incredible friends and guardians. Michael Petshaft helped me keep sane.

Gordon Davidson has been the most open-hearted and -handed producer/shepherd any playwright could ever want, and the whole staff of the Taper has been sensational, fabulous, divine.

The National Theatre staff has also been immensely supportive; and I am particularly grateful to Richard Eyre and Giles Croft for believing in the play even in its scruffiest stages.

I am also indebted to Rocco Landesman, Jack Viertel, Paul Libin, Margo Lion, Susan Gallin, Herb Alpert, Fred Zollo and the angelic hosts of brave and honorable producers who gambled on this outrageous experiment on Broadway.

Mary K. Klinger stage managed the show both in Los Angeles and in New York, unshakable in the face of many tempests.

The play has benefited from the dramaturgical work of Leon Katz and K. C. Davis, as well as the directors and actors who have participated in its various workshops and productions.

Stephen Spinella, Joe Mantello and Ellen McLaughlin have made invaluable suggestions on shaping and editing.

David Esbjornson, who directed the play in its first draft in San Francisco, has listened to and commented on its stories ever since.

Tony Taccone made invaluable structuring suggestions during his work on the play in Los Angeles.

While making the most recent revisions in the text, I've been particularly indebted to Michael Mayer, Mark Wing-Davey, Brian Kulick and Tess Timoney.

Declan Donellan and Nick Ormerod directed and designed the play at the National Theatre in London. Their early insights and responses have been challenging and helpful and have goaded me to keep trying to make the play better.

George C. Wolfe has been an inspiring and indefatigable collaborator on this final stage of shaping the script; he's been brilliantly insightful, respectful and galvanizing. The last step was the hardest, and I wouldn't have managed it without him.

Oskar Eustis commissioned *Angels in America* and has been intimately involved in every stage of its development. Without his great intelligence, talent, friendship and determination, the project would have been neither begun nor completed. I began *Angels* as a conversation, real and imaginary, between Oskar and myself; that conversation has never stopped, and never will.

A few months after I started work on *Perestroika* my mother died of cancer. She's a mighty presence in the play.

In the fifteen years of our friendship Kimberly T. Flynn has taught me much of what I now believe to be true about life: theory and practice. Her words and ideas are woven through the work, and our life together is its bedrock. *Perestroika* is for Kimberly. This is her play as much as it is mine.

THE CHARACTERS

THE ANGEL, *four divine emanations, Fluor, Phosphor, Lumen and Candle; manifest in One: the Continental Principality of America. She has magnificent gray steel wings.*

PRIOR WALTER, *Louis's abandoned boyfriend. Before discovering that he has AIDS, he occasionally worked as a club designer and caterer, mostly lives modestly off a small trust fund. Throughout* Perestroika *he has a pronounced limp, acquired in* Millennium.

HARPER AMATY PITT, *Joe's wife, an agoraphobic with a mild Valium addiction and a much stronger imagination.*

JOSEPH PORTER PITT, *chief clerk for Justice Theodore Wilson of the Federal Court of Appeals, Second Circuit.*

HANNAH PORTER PITT, *Joe's mother, formerly of Salt Lake City, now in Brooklyn, living off her deceased husband's army pension.*

BELIZE, *a former drag queen and former lover of Prior's. A registered nurse. Belize's name was originally Norman Arriaga; Belize is a drag name that stuck.*

ROY M. COHN, *a New York lawyer and unofficial power broker, now facing disbarment proceedings and dying of AIDS.*

LOUIS IRONSON, *a word processor working for the Second Circuit Court of Appeals.*

Other Characters in Part Two

ALEKSII ANTEDILLUVIANOVICH PRELAPSARIANOV, *the World's Oldest Bolshevik, played by the actor playing Hannah.*

MR. LIES, *Harper's imaginary friend, a travel agent, who in style of dress and speech suggests a jazz musician; he always wears a large lapel badge emblazoned "IOTA" (The International Order of Travel Agents). He is played by the actor playing Belize.*

HENRY, *Roy's doctor, played by the actor playing Hannah.*

ETHEL ROSENBERG, *played by the actor playing Hannah.*

EMILY, *a nurse, played by the actor playing the Angel.*

In the Diorama Room of the Mormon Visitor's Center in Act Three, the mannequins are played as follows:

THE MORMON FATHER, *played by the actor playing Joe.*

THE OFFSTAGE VOICE OF CALEB, *done by the actor playing Belize.*

THE OFFSTAGE VOICE OF ORRIN, *done by the actor playing the Angel.*

THE MORMON MOTHER, *played by the actor playing the Angel.*

In Act Five, the Continental Principalities, inconceivably powerful Celestial Apparatchik/Bureaucrat-Angels of whom the Angel of America is a peer, are played as follows:

THE ANGEL EUROPA, *played by the actor playing Joe.*

THE ANGEL AFRICANII, *played by the actor playing Harper.*

THE ANGEL OCEANIA, *played by the actor playing Belize.*

THE ANGEL ASIATICA, *played by the actor playing Hannah.*
THE ANGEL AUSTRALIA, *played by the actor playing Louis.*
THE ANGEL ANTARCTICA, *played by the actor playing Roy.*

RABBI ISIDOR CHEMELWITZ, *an orthodox Jewish rabbi, played by the actor playing Hannah.*
SARAH IRONSON, *Louis's dead grandma, whom Rabbi Chemelwitz inters in Act One of* Millennium, *played by the actor playing Louis.*
TAPED VOICE, *the voice that introduces Prelapsarianov in Act One Scene 1 and the Council of Principalities in Act Five Scene 5, and that speaks the welcome and narrative introduction in the diorama, should be that of the actor playing the Angel. These taped intros should sound alike; not parodic but beautiful and serious, the way the unseen Angel sounds in* Millennium.

Playwright's Notes

A NOTE ABOUT THE STAGING: The play benefits from a pared-down style of presentation, with minimal scenery and scene shifts done rapidly (no blackouts!) employing the cast as well as stagehands—which makes for an actor-driven event, as this must be.

The moments of magic—all of them—are to be fully realized, as bits of wonderful *theatrical* illusion—which means it's OK if the wires show, and maybe it's good that they do, but the magic should at the same time be thoroughly amazing.

(I have by now seen many productions of the two parts of *Angels*. The only ones that really succeed are the productions in which the director and designers invent great, full-blooded stage magic *for every single magical appearance and special effect.* Where this particular challenge of the plays has been shirked, the results have been disappointing and frequently ineffectual.)

It should also be said that *Millennium Approaches* and *Perestroika* are very different plays, and if one is producing them in repertory the difference should be reflected in their designs. *Perestroika* proceeds forward from the wreckage made by the Angel's traumatic entry at the end of *Millennium*. A membrane has broken; there is disarray and debris.

A NOTE TO THE ACTORS AND DIRECTORS: *Perestroika* is essentially a comedy, in that issues are resolved, mostly peaceably; growth takes place and loss is, to a certain degree, countenanced. But it's not a farce; all this happens only through a terrific amount of struggle, and the stakes are high. The Angel, the scenes in Heaven, Prior's prophet scenes are not meant to occasion lapses into some sort of elbow-in-the-ribs comedy playing style. The Angel is immensely august, serious and dangerously powerful *always*, and Prior is running for his life, sick, scared and alone. A CAUTIONARY NOTE: The play is cheapened irreparably when the actors playing the Angel and *especially* Prior fail to convey the gravity of these situations. A Prior played for laughs is death to this enterprise! Every moment must be played for its reality, the terms always life and death; only then will the comedy emerge. There is also a danger in easy sentiment. Eschew sentiment! Particularly in the final act—metaphorical though the fantasies may be (or maybe not), the problems the characters face are finally among the hardest problems—how to let go of the past, how to change and lose with grace, how to keep going in the face of overwhelming suffering. It shouldn't be easy.

A NOTE ABOUT CUTTING: The final version of *Millennium Approaches* was edited more closely than *Perestroika* has been. The text can be performed as is, or in a shorter version made by eliminating one or all three of the following passages:

Act Five, Scene 5: In the Council of Continental Principalities. The entire introduction to the scene can be eliminated, and the scene can begin with the Angel of America saying "Most August Fellow Principalities, Angels Most High: I regret my absence at this session, I was detained." If this cut is made, the taped introduction should say "*All Seven Myriad Infinite Aggregate Angelic Entities in Attendance, May Their Glorious Names Be Praised Forever and Ever, Hallelujah*" instead of "Six of Seven, etc. . . ."; the scene should begin with Prior and the Angel of America standing in the midst of the Principalities, rather than entering after the scene begins.

Act Five Scenes 6 and 9, as noted in the text, can be cut.

The elimination of these passages allows for a more streamlined final act; I feel that some of the fun and complexity of the play is lost by cutting them, but then again I have yet to see a production in which Act Five Scene 6 was kept. The decision should be made according to the specific circumstances of each production.

THE ANGEL'S COUGH: The cough is a single, dry, barking cough, not wracking emphysemic spasms. Ellen McLaughlin's cough was based on a cat hacking up a furball. It was sharp, simple and effectively nonhuman. It was not funny so much as it was ominous, and always always dignified. It is my terror that the Angel be played for laughs. She will get them, and get better laughs, if her dignity is *never* (as in not for one single second) compromised.

FLYING: If you are mounting a production of the play, and you plan to have an airborne Angel, which is a good thing, be warned: It's incredibly hard to make the flying work. Add a week to tech time.

Intermissions should be taken after Act Three and Act Four. Do not split up the acts!

A DISCLAIMER: Roy M. Cohn, the character, is based on the late Roy M. Cohn (1927–1986), who was all too real; for the most part the acts attributed to the character Roy are to be found in the historical record. But this Roy is a work of fiction; his words are my invention, and liberties have been taken with his story.

The real Roy died in August of 1986. For purposes of the play my Roy dies in February.

I want to acknowledge my indebtedness to Harold Bloom's reading of the Jacob story, which I first encountered in his introduction to Olivier Revault D'Allonnes's *Musical Variations on Jewish Thought*, in which Bloom translates the Hebrew word for "blessing" as "more life." Bloom expands on his interpretation in *The Book of J*.

Yiddish translation was graciously provided by Joachim Neugroschel, and additionally by Jeffrey Salant.

Ian Kramer, Esq. provided essential information about the juridical mischief of the Reagan-era federal bench. The court cases in Act Four Scene 8 are actual cases with some of the names and circumstances changed.

Because the soul is progressive,
it never quite repeats itself,
but in every act attempts the production
of a new and fairer whole.

—*Ralph Waldo Emerson*
"On Art"

ACT ONE:

Spooj

January 1986

Scene 1

In the darkness a Voice announces:

VOICE: In the Hall of Deputies, The Kremlin. January 1986. Aleksii Antedilluvianovich Prelapsarianov, the World's Oldest Living Bolshevik.

(Lights up on Prelapsarianov at a podium before a great red flag. He is unimaginably old and totally blind.)

ALEKSII ANTEDILLUVIANOVICH PRELAPSARIANOV: The Great Question before us is: Are we doomed? The Great Question before us is: Will the Past release us? The Great Question before us is: Can we Change? In Time? And we all desire that Change will come.
(A little pause, then with sudden, violent passion:)
And *Theory*? How are we to proceed without *Theory*? What System of Thought have these Reformers to present to this mad swirling planetary disorganization,

to the Inevident Welter of fact, event, phenomenon, calamity? Do they have, as we did, a beautiful Theory, as bold, as Grand, as comprehensive a construct . . . ? You can't imagine, when we first read the Classic Texts, when in the dark vexed night of our ignorance and terror the seed-words sprouted and shoved incomprehension aside, when the incredible bloody vegetable struggle up and through into Red Blooming gave us Praxis, True Praxis, True Theory married to Actual Life.... You who live in this Sour Little Age cannot imagine the grandeur of the prospect we gazed upon: like standing atop the highest peak in the mighty Caucasus, and viewing in one all-knowing glance the mountainous, granite order of creation. You cannot imagine it. I weep for you.

And what have you to offer now, children of this Theory? What have you to offer in its place? Market Incentives? American Cheeseburgers? Watered-down Bukharinite stopgap makeshift Capitalism! NEPmen! Pygmy children of a gigantic race!

Change? Yes, we must must change, only show me the Theory, and I will be at the barricades, show me the book of the next Beautiful Theory, and I promise you these blind eyes will see again, just to read it, to devour that text. Show me the words that will reorder the world, or else keep silent.

If the snake sheds his skin before a new skin is ready, naked he will be in the world, prey to the forces of chaos. Without his skin he will be dismantled, lose coherence and die. Have you, my little serpents, a new skin?

(A tremendous tearing and crashing sound, the great red flag is flown out; lights come up on the same tableau as at the close

of Millennium Approaches: *Prior cowering in his bed, which is strewn with the wreckage of his bedroom ceiling; and the Angel, in a gown of surpassing whiteness, barefoot and magnificent, hovering in the air, facing him.)*

AALEKSII ANTEDILLUVIANOVICH PRELAPSARIANOV: Then we dare not, we *cannot*, we MUST NOT move ahead!

ANGEL:

Greetings, Prophet.

The Great Work Begins.

The Messenger has arrived.

PRIOR: Go away.

Scene 2

The same night as the end of Millennium. *The sounds of wind and snow and magical Antarctic music; Mr. Lies is sitting alone, playing the oboe, in Harper's imaginary Antarctica. He stops playing and holds up the oboe.*

MR. LIES: The oboe: official instrument of the International Order of Travel Agents. If the duck was a songbird it would sing like this. Nasal, desolate, the call of migratory things.

(Harper enters dragging a small pine tree which she has felled. The fantasy explorer gear from Millennium *is gone; she is dressed in the hastily assembled outfit in which she fled the apartment at the end of Act Two of* Millennium; *she's been outdoors for three days now and looks it—filthy and disheveled.)*

HARPER: I'm FREEZING! IT'S TOO COLD! What happened to global warming?

MR. LIES *(Pointing to the tree):* Where did you get that?

HARPER: From the great Antarctic pine forests. Right over that hill.

MR. LIES: There are no pine forests in Antarctica.

HARPER: I chewed this pine tree down. With my teeth. Like a beaver. I'm *hungry*, I haven't eaten in three days! I'm going to use it to build . . . something, maybe a fire.

(She sits on the tree)

I don't understand why I'm not dead. When your heart breaks, you should die. But there's still the rest of you. There's your breasts, and your genitals, and they're amazingly stupid, like babies or faithful dogs, they don't get it, they just want him. Want him.

(Joe enters the scene, dressed in the overcoat and suit in which he picked up Louis in Act Three Scene 7 of Millennium. He looks around, uncertain of where he is till he sees Harper.)

MR. LIES: The Eskimo is back.

HARPER: I know. I wanted a real Eskimo, someone chilly and reliable dressed in seal pelts, not this, this is just . . . some lawyer, just . . .

JOE: Hey, buddy.

HARPER: Hey.

JOE: I looked for you. I've been everywhere.

HARPER: Well, you found me.

JOE: No, I. . . . I'm not looking now. I guess I'm having an adventure.

HARPER: Who with?

Is it fun?

JOE: Scary fun.

HARPER: Can I come with you? This isn't working anymore. I'm cold.

JOE: I wouldn't want you to see.

HARPER: Think it's worse than what I imagine? It's not.

JOE: I should go.

HARPER: Bastard. You fell out of love with me.

JOE *(Meaning it)*: That isn't true, Harper.

HARPER *(Breaking)*: THEN COME BACK!

(Little pause.)

JOE: I can't.

(He vanishes. Mr. Lies plays the oboe—a brief, wild lament. The magic Antarctic night fades away, replaced by a harsh sodium light and the ordinary sounds of the park and the city in the distance.)

MR. LIES: Blues for the death of heaven.

HARPER *(Shattered, scared)*: No!

MR. LIES: You overreached. Tore a big old hole in the sky.

HARPER: If I was a good Mormon I could have pulled it off.

MR. LIES: I tried to tell you. There are no Eskimo in Antarctica.

HARPER: No. No trees either.

MR. LIES *(Pointing to the chewed-down pine tree)*: So where did you get that?

HARPER: From the Botanical Gardens Arboretum. It's right over there. Prospect Park. We're still in Brooklyn I guess.

(The lights of a police car begin to flash.)

MR. LIES *(Vanishing)*: The Law for real.

HARPER *(Raising her arms over her head)*: Busted. Damn. What a lousy vacation.

Scene 3

In the Pitt apartment in Brooklyn. A telephone rings. Hannah, carrying the bags and wearing the coat she had on in Act Three Scene 4 of Millennium, *enters the apartment, drops the bags, runs for the phone:*

HANNAH *(Worn-out, very grim)*: Pitt residence.

No, he's out. This is his mother. No I have no idea where he is. I have no idea. He was supposed to meet me at the airport, but I don't wait more than three and three-quarters. . . . What?

OH MY LORD! Is she. . . . You. . . . Wait, officer, I don't. . . . She what? A pine tree? Why on earth would she chew a . . .

(Very severe) Well you have no business laughing about it, so you can stop that right now. That's ugly.

I don't know where that is, I just arrived from Salt Lake and I barely found Brooklyn. I'll take a . . . a taxicab. Well yes of course right now! *No.* No hospital. We don't need any of that. She's not insane, she's just peculiar.

Tell her Mother Pitt is coming.

(Hannah hangs up.)

Scene 4

Prior in bed, alone, asleep, the same night. The room is intact, no trace of the demolished ceiling. He is having a nightmare. He wakes up.

PRIOR: OH! Oh.

(He looks under the covers. He discovers that the lap of his pajamas is soaked in cum)

Fuck fuck fuck.

Will you look at this! First goddam orgasm in months and I slept through it.

(He picks up the telephone receiver, dials a number.

The phone rings by Belize's workstation on the tenth floor of New York Hospital. Belize answers.)

BELIZE: Ten East.

PRIOR: I am drenched in spooj.

BELIZE: Spooj?

PRIOR: Cum. Jiz. Ejaculate. I've had a wet dream.

BELIZE: Well about time. Miss Thing has been abstemious. She has stored up beaucoup de spooj.

PRIOR: It was a woman.

BELIZE: You turning straight on me?

PRIOR: Not a *conventional* woman.

BELIZE: Grace Jones?

(Little pause. Prior looks at the ceiling.)

BELIZE: Hello?

PRIOR: An angel.

BELIZE: Oh FABULOUS.

PRIOR: I feel . . . lascivious. Come over.

BELIZE: I spent the whole day with you, I *do* have a life of my own, you know.

PRIOR: I'm sad.

BELIZE: I thought you were lascivious.

PRIOR: Lascivious sad. Wonderful and horrible all at once, like . . . like there's a war inside. My eyes are funny, I . . .

    (He touches his eyes) Oh.

    I'm crying.

BELIZE: Prior?

PRIOR: I'm scared. And also full of, I don't know, Joy or something.

    Hope.

(In the hospital, Henry, Roy's doctor, enters.)

HENRY: Are you the duty nurse?

BELIZE: Yo.

    Look, baby, I have to go, I'll . . .

HENRY: Are you the duty nurse?

BELIZE *(To Henry)*: *Yo,* I said.

PRIOR: Sing something first. Sing with me.

HENRY: Why are you dressed like that?

BELIZE: You don't like it?

PRIOR: Just one little song. Some hymn.

HENRY: Nurses are supposed to wear white.

BELIZE: Doctors are supposed to be home, in Westchester, asleep.

    (To Prior) What hymn?

PRIOR: Ummm . . . . "Hark the Herald Angels . . ."

HENRY: *Nurse.*

BELIZE: One moment, *please.* This is an emergency.

    (To Prior, singing)

    Hark the Herald Angels sing . . .

PRIOR *(Joining in)*:

    Glory to the newborn king.

PRIOR AND BELIZE:
>Peace on earth and mercy mild,
>God and sinners reconciled . . .

HENRY *(Over the song)*: What's your name?

BELIZE *(Louder)* AND PRIOR:
>JOYFUL all ye nations rise,
>Join the triumph of the skies!
>With Angelic Hosts proclaim:
>Christ is born in Bethlehem!
>Hark the herald angels sing,
>Glory to the newborn king!

BELIZE: Call you back. There's a man bothering me.

PRIOR: Je t'aime.

(Belize hangs up.)

BELIZE: Now may I help you doctor or are you just cruising me?

HENRY: Emergency admit, Room 1013. Here are the charts. *(He hands medical charts to Belize)* Start the drip, Gamma G and he'll need a CTM, radiation in the morning so clear diet and . . .

BELIZE *(Reading the chart)*: "Liver cancer?" Oncology's on six, doll.

HENRY: This is the right floor.

BELIZE: It says liver cancer.

HENRY *(Lashing out)*: I don't give a *fuck* what it *says.* I said this is the right floor. Got it?

BELIZE: Ooooh, testy . . .

HENRY: He's a very important man.

BELIZE: Oh, OK. Then I *shouldn't* fuck up his medication?

HENRY: I'll be back in the morning.

BELIZE: Safe home.

(Henry leaves.)

BELIZE: Asshole.

(Belize picks up phone, dials; Prior answers.)

BELIZE: I have some piping hot dish.
PRIOR: How hot can it be at three in the . . . ?
BELIZE: Get out your oven mitts.
　　　　Guess who just checked in with the troubles?
　　　　The Killer Queen Herself. New York's number one closeted queer.
PRIOR: *Koch?*
BELIZE: NO! Not Koch. *(He whispers into the receiver)*
PRIOR *(Shock, then)*: The Lord moves in mysterious ways.
BELIZE: Fetch me the hammer and the pointy stake, girl. I'm a-going in.

Scene 5

Roy in his hospital bed, sick and very scared. Belize enters with the IV drip.

ROY: Get outta here you, I got nothing to say to you . . .
BELIZE: Just doing my . . .
ROY: I want a white nurse. My constitutional right.
BELIZE: You're in a hospital, you don't have any constitutional rights.

(Belize begins preparing Roy's right arm for the IV drip, palpating the vein, disinfecting the skin, etc.)

ROY *(Getting nervous about the needle)*: Find the vein, you moron, don't start jabbing that goddammed spigot in my arm till you find the fucking vein or I'll sue you so bad they'll repossess your teeth you dim black motherf . . .

BELIZE *(Had enough; very fierce)*: Watch. Yourself.

You don't talk that way to me when I'm holding something this sharp. Or I might slip and stick it in your heart. If you have a heart.

ROY: Oh I do. Tough little muscle. Never bleeds.

BELIZE: I'll bet.

Now I've been doing drips a long time. I can slip this in so easy you'll think you were born with it. Or I can make it feel like I just hooked you up to a bag of Liquid Drano. So you be nice to me or you're going to be one sorry asshole come morning.

ROY: Nice.

BELIZE: Nice and quiet.

(Belize puts the drip needle in Roy's arm.)

BELIZE: There.

ROY *(Fierce)*: I *hurt.*

BELIZE: I'll get you a painkiller.

ROY: Will it knock me out?

BELIZE: I sure hope so.

ROY: Then shove it. Pain's . . . nothing, pain's life.

BELIZE: Sing it, baby.

ROY: When they did my facelifts, I made the anesthesiologist use a local. They lifted up my whole face like a dinner napkin and I was wide awake to see it.

BELIZE: Bullshit. No doctor would agree to do that.

ROY: I can get anyone to do anything I want. For instance: Let's be friends. *(Sings)* "We shall overcome . . ."

Jews and coloreds, historical liberal coalition, right? My people being the first to sell retail to your people, your people being the first people my people could afford to hire to sweep out the store Saturday mornings, and then we all held hands and rode the bus to Selma. Not me of course, I don't ride buses, I take cabs. But the thing about the American Negro is, he never went Communist. Loser Jews did. But you people had Jesus so the reds never got to you. I admire that.

BELIZE: Your chart didn't mention that you're delusional.

ROY: Barking mad. Sit. Talk.

BELIZE: Mr. Cohn. I'd rather suck the pus out of an abscess. I'd rather drink a subway toilet. I'd rather chew off my tongue and spit it in your leathery face. So thanks for the offer of conversation, but I'd rather not.

(Belize starts to exit, turning off the light as he does.)

ROY: Oh forchristsake. Whatta I gotta do? Beg? I don't want to be alone.

(Belize stops.)

ROY: Oh how I fucking *hate* hospitals, nurses, this waste of time and . . . *wasting* and weakness, I want to kill the . . . Course they can't kill this, can they?

(Pause. Belize says nothing.)

ROY: No. It's too simple. It knows itself. It's harder to kill something if it knows what it is.

Like pubic lice. You ever have pubic lice?

BELIZE: That is none of your . . .

ROY: I got some kind of super crabs from some kid once, it took twenty drenchings of Kwell and finally shaving to get rid of the little bastards. *Nothing* could kill them. And every time I had to itch I'd smile, because I learned to respect them, these unkillable crabs, because ... I learned to identify. You know? Determined lowlife. Like me.

You've seen lots of guys with this ...

BELIZE *(Little pause, then)*: Lots.

ROY: How do I look, comparatively?

BELIZE: I'd say you're in trouble.

ROY: I'm going to die. Soon.

That was a question.

BELIZE: Probably. Probably so.

ROY: Hah.

I appreciate the ... the honesty, or whatever ...

If I live I could sue you for emotional distress, the whole hospital, but ...

I'm not prejudiced, I'm not a prejudiced man.

(Pause. Belize just looks at him.)

ROY: These racist guys, simpletons, I never had any use for them—too rigid. You want to keep your eye on where the most powerful enemy really is. I save my hate for what counts.

BELIZE: Well. And I think that's a good idea, a good thing to do, probably.

(Little pause. Then, with great effort and distaste)

This didn't come from me and I *don't* like you but let me tell you a thing or two:

They have you down for radiation tomorrow for the sarcoma lesions, and you don't want to let them do that, because radiation will kill the T-cells and you don't have

any you can afford to lose. So tell the doctor no thanks
for the radiation. He won't want to listen. Persuade him.
Or he'll kill you.

ROY: You're just a fucking nurse. Why should I listen to you
over my very qualified, very expensive WASP doctor?

BELIZE: He's not queer. I am.

(Belize winks at Roy.)

ROY: Don't wink at me.
     You said a thing or two. So that's one.

BELIZE: I don't know what strings you pulled to get in on the
azidothymidine trials.

ROY: I have my little ways.

BELIZE: Uh-huh.
     Watch out for the double blind. They'll want you to
sign something that says they can give you M&M's
instead of the real drug. You'll die, but they'll get the
kind of statistics they can publish in the *New England
Journal of Medicine*. And you can't sue cause you signed.
And if you don't sign, no pills. So if you have any strings
left, pull them, because everyone's put through the
double blind and with this, time's against you, you can't
fuck around with placebos.

ROY: You hate me.

BELIZE: Yes.

ROY: Why are you telling me this?

BELIZE: I wish I knew.

(Pause.)

ROY *(Very nasty)*: You're a butterfingers spook faggot nurse.
     I think . . . you have little reason to want to help me.

BELIZE: Consider it solidarity. One faggot to another.

(Belize snaps, turns, exits. Roy calls after him.)

ROY: Any more of your lip, boy, and you'll be flipping Big Macs in East Hell before tomorrow night!
(He picks up his bedside phone)
And get me a real phone, with a hold button, I mean look at this, it's just one little line, now how am I supposed to perform basic bodily functions on *this*?
(He thinks a minute, picks up the receiver, clicks the hang-up button several times)
Yeah who is this, the operator? Give me an outside line. Well then dial for me. It's a medical emergency darling, dial the fucking number or I'll strangle myself with the phone cord. 202-733-8525.
(Little pause)
Martin Heller. Oh hi Martin. Yeah I know what time it is, I couldn't sleep, I'm busy dying. Listen Martin, this drug they got me on, azido-methatalo-molamoca-whatchamacallit. Yeah. AZT.
I want my own private stash, Martin. Of serious Honest-Abe medicine. That I control, here in the room with me. No placebos, I'm no good at tests, Martin, I'd rather cheat. So send me my pills with a get-well bouquet, *PRONTO*, or I'll ring up CBS and sing Mike Wallace a song: *(Sotto voce, with relish)* the ballad of adorable Ollie North and his secret contra slush fund.
(He holds the phone away from his ear; Martin is excited)
Oh you only *think* you know all I know. *I* don't even know what all I know. Half the time I just make it up, and it *still* turns out to be true! We learned that trick in the fifties. Tomorrow, you two-bit scumsucking shitheel

flypaper insignificant dried-out little turd. A nice big box of drugs for Uncle Roy. Or there'll be seven different kinds of hell to pay.

(He slams the receiver down)

Scene 6

The same night. Joe and Louis at Louis's new apartment in the arctic wastes of Alphabetland; barren of furniture, unpainted, messy, grim.

Tense little pause. Louis, embarrassed, takes in the room.

LOUIS: Alphabetland. This is where the Jews lived when they first arrived. And now, a hundred years later, the place to which their more seriously fucked-up grandchildren repair. *(Yiddish accent)* This is progress?

It's a terrible mess.

JOE: It's a little dirty.

LOUIS: *Messy*, not dirty. That's an important distinction. It's dust, not dirt, chemical-slash-mineral, not organic, not like microbes, more like. . . . Can I take your tie off?

(Louis reaches towards Joe.)

JOE *(Stepping back)*: No, wait, I'm, um, um, uncomfortable, actually.

LOUIS: Me too, actually. Being uncomfortable turns me on.

JOE: Your, uh, boyfriend.

He's sick.

LOUIS: Very. He's not my boyfriend, we . . .

We can cap everything that leaks in latex, we can smear our bodies with nonoxynol-9, safe, chemical sex. Messy, but not dirty.

(Little pause)

Look I want to but I don't want to beg.

JOE: No, I . . .

LOUIS: Oh come on. *Please.*

JOE: I should go.

LOUIS: Fine! Ohblahdee, ohblahdah, life goes on. Rah.

JOE: What?

LOUIS: Hurry home to the missus.

(Pointing to Joe's left hand) Married gentlemen before cruising the Ramble should first remove their bands of gold.

Go if you're going. Go.

(Joe starts to leave. There is a moment at the door: Joe hesitating, Louis watching him. Joe goes to Louis, hugs him collegially.)

JOE: I'm not staying.

LOUIS *(Sniffing)*: What kind of cologne is that?

JOE *(A beat, then)*: Fabergé.

LOUIS: OH! *Very* butch, very heterosexual high school. Fabergé.

(Louis gently breaks the hug, steps back.)

LOUIS: You smell nice.

JOE: So do you.

LOUIS: Smell is . . . an incredibly complex and underappreciated physical phenomenon. Inextricably bound up with sex.

JOE: I . . . didn't know that.

LOUIS: It is. The nose is really a sexual organ.

Smelling. Is desiring. We have five senses, but only two
that go beyond the boundaries . . . of ourselves. When
you look at someone, it's just bouncing light, or when you
hear them, it's just sound waves, vibrating air, or touch is
just nerve endings tingling. Know what a smell is?

JOE: It's . . . some sort of. . . . No.

LOUIS: It's made of the molecules of what you're smelling.
Some part of you, where you meet the air, is airborne.
(He goes up to Joe, close)
Little molecules of Joe . . . *(He inhales deeply)* Up my
nose. Mmmm. . . . Nice. Try it.

JOE: Try . . . ?

LOUIS: Inhale.

(Joe inhales.)

LOUIS: Nice?

JOE: Yes.
I . . .

LOUIS *(Quietly)*: Ssssshhhh.
Smelling. And tasting. First the nose, then the tongue.

JOE: I just don't . . .

LOUIS: They work as a team, see. The nose tells the body—the
heart, the mind, the fingers, the cock—what it wants,
and then the tongue explores, finding out what's edible,
what isn't, what's most mineral, food for the blood, food
for the bones, and therefore most delectable.
(He licks the side of Joe's cheek)
Salt.

*(Louis kisses Joe, who holds back a moment and then
responds.)*

LOUIS: Mmm. Iron. Clay.

(Louis slips his hand down the front of Joe's pants. They embrace more tightly. Louis pulls his hand out, smells and tastes his fingers, and then holds them for Joe to smell.)

LOUIS: Chlorine. Copper. Earth.

(They kiss again.)

LOUIS: What does that taste like?
JOE: Um . . .
LOUIS: What?
JOE: Well. . . . Nighttime.
LOUIS: Stay?
JOE: Yes.
> *(Little pause)*
> Louis?
LOUIS *(Unbuttoning Joe's shirt)*: Hmmm?
JOE: What did that mean, ohblahdee ohblah . . .
LOUIS: Sssssh. Words are the worst things. Breathe. Smell.
JOE: But . . .
LOUIS: Let's stop talking. Or if you have to talk, talk dirty.

ACT TWO:

The Epistle

(For Sigrid)

February 1986

Scene 1

Prior and Belize after the funeral of a mutual friend of theirs, a major NYC drag-and-style queen. They stand outside a dilapidated funeral parlor on the Lower East Side. Belize is in defiantly bright and beautiful clothing. Prior is dressed oddly; a great long black coat and a huge, fringed, matching scarf, draped to a hoodlike effect. His appearance is disconcerting, menacing and vaguely redolent of the Biblical. (In all the scenes that follow in which Prior appears, this is his costume—he adds to and changes it slightly but it stays fundamentally corvine, ragged and eerie. It should be strange but not too strange.)

Three weeks have passed since Act One.

PRIOR: It was tacky.
BELIZE: It was divine.

He was one of the Great Glitter Queens. He couldn't be buried like a *civilian*. Trailing sequins and incense he came into the world, trailing sequins and incense he departed it. And good for him!

PRIOR: I thought the twenty professional Sicilian mourners were a bit much.

(*Little pause*)

A great queen; big fucking deal. That ludicrous spectacle in there, just a parody of the funeral of someone who *really* counted. We don't; faggots; we're just a bad dream the real world is having, and the real world's waking up. And he's *dead*.

(*Little pause.*)

BELIZE: Lately sugar you have gotten very strange. Lighten up already.

PRIOR: Oh I *apologize*, it was only a for-God's-sake funeral, a cause for fucking *celebration*, sorry if I can't join in with the rest of you death-junkies, gloating about your survival in the face of that . . . of his ugly demise because unlike you I have nothing to gloat about. Never mind.

(*Angry little pause.*)

BELIZE: And you *look* like Morticia Addams.

PRIOR: Like the Wrath of God.

BELIZE: Yes.

PRIOR: That is the intended effect.

My eyes are fucked up.

BELIZE: Fucked up how?

PRIOR: Everything's . . . closing in. Weirdness on the periphery.

BELIZE: Since when?

PRIOR: For three weeks. Since that night. Since the night when . . . (*He stops himself*)

BELIZE: Well what does the eye doctor say?

PRIOR: I haven't been.

BELIZE: Oh for *God's sake.* Why?

PRIOR: I was improving. Before.

Remember my wet dream.

BELIZE: The angel?

PRIOR: It wasn't a dream.

BELIZE: Course it was.

PRIOR: No. I don't think so. I think it really happened.

I'm a prophet.

BELIZE: Say what?

PRIOR: I've been given a prophecy. A book. Not a *physical* book, or there was one but they took it back, but somehow there's still this book. In me. A prophecy. It . . . really happened, I'm . . . almost completely sure of it.

(He looks at Belize)

Oh stop looking so . . .

BELIZE: You're scaring me.

PRIOR: It was after Louis left me. Every night I'd been having these horrible vivid dreams. And then . . .

(Little pause.)

BELIZE: Then . . . ?

PRIOR: And then She arrived.

Scene 2

The Angel and Prior in Prior's bedroom, three weeks earlier: the wrecked ceiling. Prior moves to the bed (changing into his PJ's—he should take his time doing this), the Angel in the air. Belize watches from the street.

ANGEL:

> Greetings, Prophet!
> The Great Work Begins:
> The Messenger has arrived.

PRIOR: Go away.

ANGEL:

> Attend:

PRIOR: Oh God there's a thing in the air, a thing, a thing.

ANGEL:

> I I I I
> Am the Bird Of America, the Bald Eagle,
> Continental Principality,
> LUMEN PHOSPHOR FLUOR CANDLE!
> I unfold my leaves, Bright steel,
> In salutation open sharp before you:
> PRIOR WALTER
> Long-descended, well-prepared . . .

PRIOR: No, I'm not prepared, for anything, I have lots to do,
   I . . .

ANGEL (*With another gust of music*):

> American Prophet tonight you become,
> American Eye that pierceth Dark,
> American Heart all Hot for Truth,
> The True Great Vocalist, the Knowing Mind,
> Tongue-of-the-Land, Seer-Head!

PRIOR: Oh, Shoo! You're scaring the shit out of me, get the
   fuck out of my room. Please, oh please . . .

ANGEL:

> Now:
> Remove from their hiding place the Sacred Prophetic
>   Implements.

(Little pause.)

PRIOR: The *what?*

ANGEL:

> Remove from their hiding place the Sacred Prophetic
> Implements.
> *(Little pause)*
> Your dreams have revealed them to you.

PRIOR: What dreams?

ANGEL: You have had dreams revealing to you . . .

PRIOR: I haven't had a dream I can remember in months.

ANGEL: No . . . dreams, you. . . . Are you sure?

PRIOR: Yes. Well, the two dead Priors, they . . .

ANGEL: No not the heralds, not them. Other dreams. Implements, you must have. . . . One moment.

PRIOR: *This,* this is a dream, obviously, I'm sick and so I. . . . Well OK it's a pretty spectacular dream but still it's just some . . .

ANGEL: Quiet. Prophet. A moment, please, I. . . . The disorganization is . . .

> *(She coughs, looks up)* He says he hasn't had any . . .
> *(Coughs)*
> Yes.
> In the kitchen. Under the tiles under the sink.

PRIOR: You want me to . . . to tear up the kitchen floor?

ANGEL: Get a shovel or an axe or some . . . tool for dislodging tile and grout and unearth the Sacred Implements.

PRIOR: No fucking way! The ceiling's bad enough, I'll lose the lease, I'll lose my security deposit, I'll wake up the downstairs neighbors, their hysterical dog, I. . . . Do it yourself.

ANGEL *(A really terrifying voice)*: SUBMIT, SUBMIT TO THE WILL OF HEAVEN!

(An enormous gust of wind knocks Prior over. He glares at Her from the floor and shakes his head "no." A standoff. The

Angel coughs a little. There is a small, soft explosion in the kitchen offstage. A cloud of plaster dust drifts on.)

PRIOR: What did you. . . . What . . . ? *(Exits into the kitchen)*

ANGEL: And Lo, the Prophet was led by his nightly dreams to the hiding place of the Sacred Implements, and. . . . Revision in the text: The Angel did help him to unearth them, for he was weak of body though not of will.

(Prior returns with an ancient leather suitcase, very dusty.)

PRIOR: You cracked the refrigerator, you probably released a whole cloud of fluorocarbons, that's bad for the . . . the environment.

ANGEL: My wrath is as fearsome as my countenance is splendid. Open the suitcase.

(Prior does. He reaches inside and produces a pair of bronze spectacles with rocks instead of lenses.)

PRIOR: Oh, look at this. *(He puts them on)*
    Like, wow, man, totally Paleozoic. This is . . .
    (He stops suddenly. His head jerks up. He is seeing something)
    OH! OH GOD NO! OH . . . *(He rips off the spectacles)*
    That was terrible! I don't want to see that!

ANGEL: Remove the Book.

(Prior removes a large book with bright steel pages from the suitcase. There is a really glorious burst of music, more light, more wind.)

ANGEL:

> From the Council of Continental Principalities
> Met in this time of Crisis and Confusion:
> Heaven here reaches down to disaster
> And in touching you touches all of Earth.

(Music. She retrieves the spectacles, gives them to him.)

ANGEL:

> Peep-stones.

(He cautiously puts them on as:)

ANGEL:

> Open me Prophet. I I I I am
> The Book.
> Read.

PRIOR: Wait. Wait. *(He takes off the glasses)*
How come. . . . How come I have this . . . um, erection? It's very hard to concentrate.

ANGEL: The stiffening of your penis is of no consequence.

PRIOR: Well maybe not to you but . . .

ANGEL:

> READ!
> You are Mere Flesh. I I I I am Utter Flesh,
> Density of Desire, the Gravity of Skin:
> What makes the Engine of Creation Run?
> Not Physics But Ecstatics Makes the Engine Run:

(The Angel's lines are continuous through this section. Prior's lines overlap. They both get very turned-on.)

PRIOR *(Hit by a wave of intense sexual feeling)*: Hmmmm . . .

ANGEL:

> The Pulse, the Pull, the Throb, the Ooze . . .

PRIOR: Wait, please, I. . . . Excuse me for just a minute, just a minute. . . . OK I . . .

ANGEL:

> Priapsis, Dilation, Engorgement, Flow:
> The Universe Aflame with Angelic Ejaculate . . .

PRIOR *(Losing control, he starts to hump the Book)*: Oh shit . . .

ANGEL:

> The Heavens A-thrum to the Seraphic Rut,
> The Fiery Grapplings . . .

PRIOR: Oh God, I . . .

ANGEL:

> The Feathery Joinings of the Higher Orders,
> Infinite, Unceasing, the Blood-Pump of Creation!

PRIOR: OH! OH! I. . . . OH! Oh! Oh, oh . . .

ANGEL *(Simultaneously)*: HOLY Estrus! HOLY Orifice! Ecstasis in Excelsis! AMEN!

(Pause.)

PRIOR: Oh. Oh God.

ANGEL:

> The Body is the Garden of the Soul.

PRIOR: What *was* that?

ANGEL:

> Plasma Orgasmata.

PRIOR: Yeah well no doubt.

BELIZE: Whoa whoa whoa wait a minute excuse me please. You fucked this angel?

PRIOR: She fucked me. She has . . . well, she has eight vaginas.

ANGEL:

> REGINA VAGINA!

Hermaphroditically Equipped as well with a Bouquet
of Phallī . . .

I I I I am Your Released Female Essence Ascendant.

PRIOR *(To Belize)*: The sexual politics of this are *very* confusing. God, for example is a man. Well, not a man, he's
a flaming Hebrew letter, but a male flaming Hebrew
letter.

ANGEL:

The Aleph Glyph. Deus Erectus! Pater Omnipotens!

PRIOR: Angelic orgasm makes protomatter, which fuels the
Engine of Creation. They used to copulate *ceaselessly*
before . . .

Each angel is an infinite aggregate myriad entity,
they're basically incredibly powerful bureaucrats, they
have no imagination, they can *do* anything but they can't
invent, create, they're sort of fabulous and dull all at once:

ANGEL:

Made for His Pleasure, We can only ADORE:
Seeking something New . . .

PRIOR:

God split the World in Two . . .

ANGEL:

And made *YOU*:

PRIOR AND ANGEL:

Human Beings:
Uni-Genitaled: Female. Male.

ANGEL:

In creating You, Our Father-Lover unleashed
Sleeping Creation's Potential for Change.
In YOU the Virus of TIME began!

PRIOR: In making people God apparently set in motion a
potential in the design for change, for random event, for
movement forward.

ANGEL:

> YOU *Think*. And You *IMAGINE*!
>
> Migrate, Explore, and when you do:

PRIOR: As the human race began to progress, travel, intermingle, everything started to come unglued. Manifest first as tremors in Heaven.

ANGEL:

> Heaven is a city Much Like San Francisco.
>
> House upon house depended from Hillside,
>
> From Crest down to Dockside,
>
> The green Mirroring Bay:

PRIOR: And there are earthquakes there, or rather, heaven-quakes.

ANGEL:

> Oh Joyful in the Buckled Garden:
>
> Undulant Landscape Over which
>
> The Threat of Seismic Catastrophe hangs:
>
> More beautiful because imperiled.
>
> POTENT: yet DORMANT: the Fault Lines of Creation!

BELIZE: So Human progress . . .

PRIOR: Migration. Science. Forward Motion.

BELIZE: . . . shakes up Heaven.

ANGEL:

> Paradise itself Shivers and Splits,
>
> Each day when You awake, as though WE Are only the Dream of YOU.
>
> PROGRESS! MOVEMENT!
>
> Shaking *HIM*:

BELIZE: God.

ANGEL:

> He began to leave Us!
>
> Bored with His Angels, Bewitched by Humanity,

In Mortifying imitation of You, his least creation,
He would sail off on Voyages, no knowing where.
Quake follows quake,
Absence follows Absence:
Nasty Chastity and Disorganization:
Loss of Libido, Protomatter Shortfall:
We are his Functionaries; It is
BEYOND US:
Then:
April 18, 1906.
In That Day:

PRIOR: The Great San Francisco Earthquake. And also . . .

ANGEL:

In that day:

PRIOR *(Simultaneously)*: On April 18, 1906 . . .

ANGEL:

Our Lover of the Million Unutterable Names,
The Aleph Glyph from Which all Words Descend:
The King of the Universe:
HE Left . . .

PRIOR: Abandoned.

ANGEL:

And did not return.
We do not know where HE has gone. HE may *never . . .*
And bitter, cast-off, We wait, bewildered;
Our finest houses, our sweetest vineyards,
Made drear and barren, missing Him.
(Coughs)

BELIZE: Abandoned.

PRIOR: Yes.

BELIZE: I smell a motif. The man that got away.

PRIOR: Well it occurred to me. Louis.

(Very sad) Even now, if he came back I'd . . . *(He shrugs)*

BELIZE: Listen to your girlfriend.

> I think the time has come to let him go.

PRIOR: That's not what the angels think, they think. . . . It's all gone too far, too much loss is what they think, we should stop somehow, go back.

BELIZE: But that's not how the world works, Prior. It only spins forward.

PRIOR: Yeah but forward into *what*?

ANGEL:

> Surely you see towards what We are Progressing:
> The fabric of the sky unravels:
> Angels hover, anxious fingers worry
> The tattered edge.
> Before the boiling of blood and the searing of skin
> Comes the Secret catastrophe:
> Before Life on Earth becomes finally merely
> impossible,
> It will for a long time before have become completely
> unbearable.
> *(Coughs)*
> *YOU HAVE DRIVEN HIM AWAY!* YOU MUST
> STOP MOVING!

PRIOR *(Quiet, terrified)*: Stop moving.

ANGEL *(Softly)*:

> Forsake the Open Road:
> Neither Mix Nor Intermarry: Let Deep Roots Grow:
> If you do not MINGLE you will Cease to Progress:
> Seek Not to Fathom the World and its Delicate
> Particle Logic:
> You cannot Understand, You can only Destroy,
> You do not Advance, You only Trample.
> Poor blind Children, abandoned on the Earth,
> Groping terrified, misguided, over

Fields of Slaughter, over bodies of the Slain:
HOBBLE YOURSELVES!
There is No Zion Save Where You Are!
If you Cannot find your Heart's desire . . .

PRIOR: In your own backyard . . .

ANGEL, PRIOR AND BELIZE: You never lost it to begin with.

(The Angel coughs.)

ANGEL:

Turn Back. Undo.
Till HE returns again.

PRIOR: Please. Please. Whatever you are, I don't understand this visitation, I'm not a prophet, I'm a sick, lonely man, I don't understand what you want from me.

(The Angel picks up the Book.)

PRIOR: Stop moving. That's what you want. Answer me! You want me dead.

(Pause. The Angel and Prior look at each other.)

ANGEL: No more.

PRIOR: *I. WANT.* You to go away. I'm tired to death of being done to, walked out on, *infected*, fucked over and *now* tortured by some mixed-up, reactionary angel, some . . .

(The Angel lands in front of Prior.)

ANGEL:

You can't Outrun your Occupation, Jonah.
Hiding from Me one place you will find me in
    another.
I I I I stop down the road, waiting for you.

(She touches him, tenderly, and turns him, cradling him with one arm.)

ANGEL:

You Know Me Prophet: Your battered heart,
Bleeding Life in the Universe of Wounds.

(The Angel presses the volume against his chest. They both experience something unnameable—painful, joyful in equal measure. There is a terrifying sound. The Angel gently, lovingly lowers Prior to the ground.)

ANGEL:

Vessel of the BOOK now: Oh Exemplum Paralyticum:
On you in you in your blood we write have written:
STASIS!
The END.

(In gales of music, holding the Book aloft, the Angel ascends. The bedroom disappears. Prior stands, puts on his street clothes and resumes his place beside Belize. They are back on the street in front of the funeral home.)

BELIZE: You have been spending too much time alone.

PRIOR: Not by choice. None of this by choice.

BELIZE: This is . . . worse than nuts, it's . . . well, don't migrate, don't mingle, that's . . . malevolent, some of us didn't exactly *choose* to migrate, know what I'm saying . . .

PRIOR *(Overlapping)*: I hardly think it's appropriate for you to get *offended*, I didn't invent this shit it was *visited* on me . . .

BELIZE *(Overlapping on "offended")*: But it *is* offensive or at least monumentally confused and it's not . . . *visited*, Prior. By who? It *is* from you, what else is it?

PRIOR: Something else.

BELIZE: That's crazy.

PRIOR: Then I'm crazy.

BELIZE: No, you're . . .

PRIOR: Then it was an angel.

BELIZE: It was *not* an . . .

PRIOR: Then I'm crazy. The whole world is, why not me?

It's 1986 and there's a *plague*, half my friends are dead and I'm only thirty-one, and every goddamn morning I wake up and I think Louis is next to me in the bed and it takes me long minutes to remember . . . that this is *real*, it isn't just an impossible, terrible dream, so maybe yes I'm flipping out.

BELIZE *(Angry)*: You better not. You better fucking not flip out.

This is not dementia. And this is not real. This is just you, Prior, afraid of what's coming, afraid of time. But see that's just not how it goes, the world doesn't spin backwards. Listen to the world, to how fast it goes.

(They stand silently, listening, and the sounds of the city grow louder and louder, filling the stage—sounds of traffic, whistles, alarms, people, all very fast and very complex and very determinedly moving ahead.)

BELIZE: That's New York traffic, baby, the sound of energy, the sound of time. Even if you're hurting, it can't go back.

There's no angel. You hear me? For me? I can handle anything but not this happening to you.

ANGEL'S VOICE:

Whisper into the ear of the World, Prophet,
Wash up red in the tide of its dreams,
And billow bloody words into the sky of sleep.

PRIOR: Maybe I am a prophet. Not just me, all of us who are dying now. Maybe we've caught the virus of prophecy. Be still. Toil no more. Maybe the world has driven God from Heaven, incurred the angels' wrath.

I believe I've seen the end of things. And having seen, I'm going blind, as prophets do. It makes a certain sense to me.

ANGEL'S VOICE:

FOR THIS AGE OF ANOMIE: A NEW LAW!
Delivered this night, this silent night, from Heaven, Oh Prophet, to You.

PRIOR: I hate heaven. I've got no resistance left. Except to run.

ACT THREE:

Borborygmi

(The Squirming Facts Exceed the Squamous Mind)

February 1986

Scene 1

> *Split scene: a week later, a month since the end of Act One. Joe and Louis in bed, different sheets, tidier, homier. Joe is awake, Louis is asleep. Joe watches Harper, in Brooklyn, dressed in a soiled nightgown. She removes her nightgown and stands shivering in bra and panties and stockings, looking at Joe. Hannah enters in a bathrobe, carrying a dress over her arm and a pair of shoes. She puts the shoes down in front of Harper.*

HANNAH: Did you wash up?

(Harper nods.)

HANNAH: Good you're out of that nightdress, it's been three weeks. It was starting to smell.
HARPER *(Flat)*: You're telling me.
HANNAH: Now let's slip this on.

(They put the dress on Harper.)

HANNAH: Good. It's pretty.
    Shoes?

(Harper steps into them.)

HANNAH: Good. Now let's see about the hair.

(Harper bends over; Hannah combs Harper's hair.)

HANNAH: At first it can be very hard to accept how disap-
    pointing life is, Harper, because that's what it is and you
    have to accept it. With faith and time and hard work you
    reach a point . . . where the disappointment doesn't hurt
    as much, and then it gets actually easy to live with. Quite
    easy. Which is in its own way a disappointment. But.
    There.
HARPER: I hate this dress, Mother Pitt. It's five AM.
HANNAH: I get there first. I open up.
    I leave messages at work. They say he's not in but I
    know he is, but he won't take my calls. He's ashamed.

(Harper stares at Joe.)

HARPER: I miss his penis.
HANNAH: And I'm sure you'll understand if I don't feel com-
    fortable discussing that.
    I'll fix myself now. And we can go.

(Hannah exits.)

HARPER: Joe?

(She crosses into Louis's bedroom. Joe pulls back, away from her but careful not to wake Louis.)

HARPER: Don't worry, I'm not really here.

    I have terrible powers. I see more than I want to see. Maybe I'm a witch.

JOE: You're not.

HARPER: I could be a witch. Why not? I married a fairy.

JOE: Please, Harper, go, just . . .

LOUIS *(Waking but not really)*: Joe . . . ?

    You OK?

JOE: Yeah, yeah, screwy stomach, nothing.

HARPER *(Simultaneously)*: Talk softer you're waking him up.

    Why am I here? You called me.

JOE: I didn't . . .

HARPER: You called me. Leave me alone if you're so goddamned happy.

JOE: I didn't call you.

HARPER: THEN WHY AM I HERE?

(Pause. They look at each other.)

HARPER: To see you again. Any way I can.

    OH GOD I WISH YOU WERE. . . . No I don't. DEAD. Yes, I do.

LOUIS: Joe . . . ?

HARPER: You love him.

JOE: I do?

HARPER: You can't save him. You never saved anyone. Joe in love, isn't it pathetic.

JOE: What?

HARPER: You're turning into me.

JOE: GO!

(She vanishes as Louis wakes with a start.)

LOUIS: What!?

JOE: Morning.

Sleep well?

LOUIS: No. Did you?

JOE: Yup.

LOUIS: I had a freaky nightmare. We were celebrating having spent a month in bed and we'd decided to meet at a restaurant, only I wasn't sure it was right to be celebrating and when I got there it wasn't a restaurant, it was the funeral parlor of some sort of creepy temple, and it was you and me and some furiously angry woman, and it turned out that you were a member of some bizarre religious sect, like a Moonie or a Rajnishi or a Mormon or something, and you hadn't told me, and it was like I didn't know you at all.

Joe?

(Little pause, Joe stares at Louis.)

JOE: I am. I am a Mormon.

LOUIS *(A beat, then)*: Huh.

Scene 2

Same morning, still five AM. Roy in his hospital room. The pain in his gut is now constant and getting worse. He is on the phone, a more elaborate phone than in the previous scene.

ROY: No records no records what are you deaf I said I have no records for their shitty little committee, it's not how I work I . . .

(He has an incredibly bad abdominal spasm; he's in great pain. He holds the phone away, grimaces terribly, curls up into a ball and then uncurls, all the while making no sound.
    Ethel appears in her hat and coat, walks to a chair by the bed and sits, watching Roy, silent. He watches her enter and then resumes his phone call, never taking his eyes off her.)

ROY: Those notes were lost. LOST. In a fire, water damage, I can't do this any . . .

(Belize enters with a pill tray.)

ROY *(To Belize)*: I threw up fifteen times today! I *COUNTED*.
    (Pause. To Ethel) What are *you* looking at?
    (To Belize) Fifteen times. *(He goes back to the phone)* Yeah?
BELIZE: Hang up the phone, I have to watch you take these . . .
ROY: The LIMO thing? Oh for the love of Christ I was acquitted twice for that, they're trying to kill me dead with this *harassment*, I have done things in my life but I never killed anyone.
    (To Ethel) Present company excepted. And you *deserved* it.
    (To Belize) Get the fuck outta here.
    (Back to the phone) Stall. It can't start tomorrow if we don't show, so don't show, I'll pay the old harridan back. I have to have a . . .
BELIZE: Put down the phone.

ROY: Suck my dick, Mother Teresa, this is life and death.

BELIZE: Put down the . . .

(Roy snatches the pill cup off the tray and throws the pills on the floor. Belize reaches for the phone. Roy slams down the receiver and snatches the phone away.)

ROY: You touch that phone and I'll bite. And I got rabies.

And from now on, I supply my own pills. I already told 'em to push their jujubes to the losers down the hall.

BELIZE: Your own pills.

ROY: No double blind. A little bird warned me. The vultures . . .

(Another severe spasm. This time he makes noise) Jesus God these cramps, now I know why women go beserk once a. . . . AH FUCK!

(He has another spasm. Ethel laughs.)

ROY: Oh good I made her laugh.

(The pain is slightly less. He's a little calmer)

I don't trust this hospital. For all I know Lillian fucking *Hellman* is down in the basement switching the pills around—no, wait, she's dead, isn't she. Oh boy, memory, it's—hey Ethel, didn't Lillian die, did you see her up there, ugly, ugly broad, nose like a . . . like even a Jew should worry mit a punim like that. You seen somebody fitting that description up there in Red Heaven? Hah?

She won't talk to me. She thinks she's some sort of a deathwatch or something.

BELIZE: Who are you talking to?

ROY: I'm self-medicating.

BELIZE: With what?

ROY *(Trying to remember)*: Acid something.

BELIZE: Azidothymedine?

ROY: Gesundheit.

(Roy tosses a ring of keys to Belize.)

BELIZE: AZT? You got. . . ?

(Belize unlocks the ice box; it's full of bottles of pills.)

ROY: One-hundred-proof elixir vitae.

Give me the keys.

BELIZE: You scored.

ROY: Impressively.

BELIZE: Lifetime supply.

There are maybe thirty people in the whole country who are getting this drug.

ROY: Now there are thirty-one.

BELIZE: There are a hundred thousand people who need it.

Look at you. The dragon atop the golden horde. It's not fair, is it?

ROY: No, but as Jimmy Carter said, neither is life. So put your brown eyes back in your goddam head, baby, I am not moved by an unequal distribution of goods on this earth. It's history, I didn't write it though I flatter myself I am a footnote. And you are a nurse, so minister and skedaddle.

BELIZE: If you live fifty more years you won't swallow all these pills.

(Pause)

I want some.

ROY: That's illegal.

BELIZE: Ten bottles.

ROY: I'm gonna report you.

BELIZE: There's a nursing shortage. I'm in a union. I'm real
scared.

I have friends who need them. Bad.

ROY: Loyalty I admire. But no.

BELIZE *(Amazed, off guard)*: Why?

(Pause.)

ROY: Because you repulse me. "*WHY?*" You'll be begging for
it next. "*WHY?*" Because I hate your guts, and your
friends' guts, that's *why*. "Gimme!" So goddamned entitled. Such a shock when the bill comes due.

BELIZE: From what I read you never paid a fucking bill in your
life.

ROY: *No one* has worked harder than me. To end up knocked
flat in a . . .

BELIZE: Yeah well things are tough all over.

ROY: And you come *here* looking for *fairness*? *(To Ethel)* They
couldn't *touch* me when I was alive, and now when I am
dying they try this: *(He grabs up all the paperwork in two
fists)* Now! When I'm a . . . *(Back to Belize)* That's fair?
What am I? A dead man!

(A terrible spasm, quick and violent; he doubles up)

Fuck! What was I saying Oh God I can't remember
any. . . . Oh yeah, dead.

I'm a goddam dead man.

BELIZE: You expect *pity*?

ROY *(A beat, then)*: I expect you to hand over those keys and
move your nigger ass out of my room.

BELIZE: What did you say.

ROY: Move your nigger cunt spade faggot lackey ass out of my
room.

BELIZE *(Overlapping starting on "spade")*: Shit-for-brains filthy-mouthed selfish motherfucking cowardly cock-sucking cloven-hoofed pig.

ROY *(Overlapping)*: Mongrel. Dinge. Slave. Ape.

BELIZE: Kike.

ROY: *Now* you're talking!

BELIZE: Greedy kike.

ROY: Now you can have a bottle. But only one.

(Belize tosses the keys at Roy, hard. Roy catches them. Belize takes a bottle of the pills, then another, then a third, and leaves.

As soon as Belize is out of the room Roy is wracked with a series of spasms; he's been holding them in.)

ROY: GOD I thought he'd never go!

(To Ethel) So what? Are you going to sit there all night?

ETHEL: Till morning.

ROY: Uh huh. The cock crows, you go back to the swamp.

ETHEL: No. I take the 7:05 to Yonkers.

ROY: What the fuck's in Yonkers?

ETHEL: The disbarment committee hearings. You been hocking about it all week. I'll have a look-see.

ROY: They won't let you in the front door. You're a convicted and executed traitor.

ETHEL: I'll walk through a wall.

(She starts to laugh. He joins her.)

ROY: Fucking SUCCUBUS! Fucking bloodsucking old bat!

(Roy picks up the phone, punches a couple of buttons and then puts the receiver back, dejectedly)

The worst thing about being sick in America, Ethel, is you are booted out of the parade. Americans have no use for sick. Look at Reagan: He's so healthy he's hardly human, he's a hundred if he's a day, he takes a slug in his chest and two days later he's out west riding ponies in his PJ's. I mean who does that? That's America. It's just no country for the infirm.

Scene 3

Later the same day. The Diorama Room of the Mormon Visitor's Center. The diorama is in a little proscenium theatre; the curtains are drawn shut. Behind them is a classic wagon-train tableau posed before a painted backdrop: a covered wagon and a Mormon family in the desert on the great trek from Missouri to Salt Lake. The family members are historically dressed mannequins: two sons, a mother and a daughter, and the father (who is actually the actor playing Joe). There are nice seats for the audience; and Harper is in one of them, dressed the same as in her last scene. She has bags of potato chips and M&M's and cans of soda scattered all around. Hannah enters with Prior.

HANNAH: This is the Diorama Room.
     (To Harper) I thought we agreed that you weren't . . .
     (To Prior) I'll go see if I can get it started.

(She exits. Prior sits. The lights in the room dim. A Voice on tape intones:)

VOICE: Welcome to the Mormon Visitor's Center Diorama Room. In a moment, our show will begin. We hope it will have a special message for you. Please refrain from smoking, and food and drink are not allowed. *(A chiming tone)* Welcome to the Mormon Visitor's . . .

(The tape lurches into very high speed, then smears into incomprehensibly low speed, then stops, mid-message, with an unpromising metallic blat, which frightens Prior.)

HARPER: They're having trouble with the machinery.

(She rips open a bag of nacho-flavored Doritos and offers them to Prior.)

PRIOR: You're not supposed to eat in the . . .
HARPER: I can. I live here. Have we met before?
PRIOR: No, I don't . . . think so. You *live* here?
HARPER *(Pointing to the father dummy)*: There's a dummy family in the diorama, you'll see when the curtain opens. The main dummy, the big daddy dummy, looks like my husband, Joe. When they push the buttons he'll start to talk. You can't believe a word he says but the sound of him is reassuring. It's an *incredible* resemblance.
PRIOR: Are you a Mormon?
HARPER: Jack Mormon.
PRIOR: I beg your pardon?
HARPER: Jack Mormon. It means I'm flawed. Inferior Mormon product. Probably comes from jack rabbit, you know, I *ran*.
PRIOR: Do you believe in angels? In the Angel Mormon?
HARPER: Moroni, not Mormon, the Angel Moroni. Ask my mother-in-law, when you leave, the scary lady at the reception desk, if its name was Moroni why don't they call themselves Morons. It's from comments like that you can tell I'm jack Mormon. You're not a Mormon.

PRIOR: No, I . . .

HARPER: Just . . . distracted with grief.

PRIOR: I'm not. I was just walking and . . .

HARPER: We get a lot of distracted, grief-stricken people here. It's our specialty.

PRIOR: I'm not . . . distracted, I'm doing research.

HARPER: On Mormons?

PRIOR: On. . . . Angels. I'm a. . . . An angelologist.

HARPER: I never met an angelologist before.

PRIOR: It's an obscure discipline.

HARPER: I can imagine. Angelology. The field work must be rigorous. You'd have to drop dead before you saw your first specimen.

PRIOR: One. . . . I saw one. An angel. It crashed through my bedroom ceiling.

HARPER: Huh. That sort of thing always happens to me.

PRIOR: I have a fever. I should be in bed but I'm too anxious to lie in bed. You look *very* familiar.

HARPER: So do you.

But it's just not possible. I don't get out. I've only ever been here, or in some place a lot like this, alone, in the dark, waiting for the dummy.

(The lights in the Diorama Room darken; dramatic music; the curtains part and lights come up on the little stage. The Voice on tape again:)

VOICE: In 1847, across fifteen hundred miles of frontier wilderness, braving mountain blizzards, desert storms, and renegade Indians, the first Mormon wagon trains made their difficult way towards the Kingdom of God.

HARPER: Want some nacho-flavored. . . . Hi Joe.

(The diorama comes to life. Sounds of a wagon train, the Largo from Dvorak's Ninth Symphony. The boy dummies, Caleb and Orrin, don't talk, you just hear their voices on a tape, and a pinspot hits their faces to indicate who is talking: the effect is unintentionally eerie. The father's face moves but not his body.)

CALEB *(Voice on tape)*: Father, I'm a-feard.

FATHER: Hush, Caleb.

ORRIN *(Voice on tape)*: The wilderness is so vast.

FATHER: Orrin, Caleb, hush. Be brave for your mother and your little sister.

CALEB:
We'll try, father, we want you to be proud of us. We want to be brave and strong like you.

ORRIN:
When will we arrive in Zion, father? When will our great exodus finally be done? All this wandering . . .

FATHER:
Soon boys, soon, just like the Prophet promised. The Lord leads the way.

HARPER:
They don't have any lines, the sister and the mother. And only his face moves. That's not really fair.

HARPER:
Never. You'll die of snake bite and your brother looks like scorpion food to me.

PRIOR:
Sssshhhh . . .

CALEB:
Will there be lots to eat
there, Father? Will the desert
flow with milk and honey? Will
there be water there?

FATHER:
The Lord will provide for
us, son, he always has.

ORRIN:
Well, not *always* . . .

FATHER:
Sometimes He tests us, son,
that's His way, but . . .

HARPER:
No.
Just sand.
(On"water")
Oh, there's a big lake
but it's *salt*, that's the
joke, they drag you on
your knees through hell
and when you get there
the water of course is
undrinkable. Salt.
It's a Promised land, but
what a disappointing
promise!

CALEB: Read to us, father, read us the story!
FATHER *(Chuckles)*: *Again?*

SONS:
Yes! Yes! The Story! The
Story! The story about the
Prophet!

HARPER:
The story! The story!
The story about the
Prophet!

FATHER: Well boys, well:
  1823, the Prophet, who was a strapping lad, like everyone else in his time was seeking God, there were many
churches, disputatious enough but who was Right?
Could only be One True Church. All else darkness . . .

(Louis suddenly appears in the diorama.)

LOUIS: OK yeah yeah yeah but then answer me this: How can
a fundamentalist theocratic religion function participa-
torily in a pluralist secular democracy? Are you busy?
JOE: Well, I'm working, but . . .
LOUIS: I can't *believe* you're a Mormon! I can't believe I've
spent a month in bed with a Mormon!
JOE: Um, could you talk a little softer, I . . .
LOUIS: But you're a lawyer! A *serious* lawyer!

PRIOR:	JOE:
Oh my god Oh my god.	The chief clerk of
What. . . . What is going on here?	the Chief Justice of the
	Supreme Court is a
HARPER:	Mormon, Louis, please
You know him?	don't let's argue now, we
	can talk at home tonight . . .

PRIOR *(Closing his eyes)*: I'm delirious, I must be delirious.
LOUIS: I don't like cults.
JOE: The Church of Jesus Christ of Latter Day Saints is not a
cult.
LOUIS: Any religion that's not at least two thousand years old
is a cult.

PRIOR:	JOE:
WHAT IS HE DOING	Come here, Louis . . .
IN THERE?	

LOUIS: And I know people who would call *that* generous.
I hate it when you ignore that I'm being obnoxious.
PRIOR: WHAT IS HE . . .
HARPER: Who? The little creep? He's in and out every day.
I hate him. He's got absolutely *nothing* to do with the story.

(Joe kisses Louis.)

PRIOR Can you turn it off? The. . . . I'm leaving, I can't . . .

LOUIS: Why didn't you tell me that you . . .

JOE: It's a surprise?

LOUIS: No, no most of the men I go to bed with turn out to be YEAH OF COURSE it's a surprise! I thought you were all out west somewhere with the salt flats and the cactuses. There's some sort of profound displacement going on here, I . . .

PRIOR: Louis . . .

LOUIS *(Hearing him)*: Did you . . .

JOE: What?

LOUIS: I thought I heard. . . . Somebody. Prior.
     (To Joe) We have to talk.

JOE: But I can't just leave the office.

LOUIS: Fuck it! This is a crisis. Now.

(Louis exits. Joe sighs and then follows.)

HARPER: Well the dummy never *left* with the little creep, he never left before. When they come in and they see he's gone, they'll blame me.

(Harper goes to the diorama stage and pulls its bright red velvet curtain closed. She turns back and sees that Prior is crying.)

HARPER: You shouldn't do that in here, this isn't a place for real feelings, this is just storytime here, stop.

PRIOR: I never imagined losing my mind was going to be such hard work.

HARPER: Oh, it is.

Find someplace else to be miserable in. This is *my* place and I don't want you to do that here!

PRIOR: I JUST SAW MY LOVER, MY . . . ex-lover, with a . . . with your husband, with that . . . window-display Ken doll, in that . . . *thing*, I saw him, I . . .

HARPER: Well don't have a hissy fit, I told you it wasn't working right, it's just . . . the magic of the theatre or something. Listen, if you see the creep, tell him to bring Joe . . . to bring the mannequin back, they'll evict me and this is it, it's nothing but it's the last place on earth for me. I can't go sit in Brooklyn.

(Hannah enters.)

HANNAH: What's all the . . .
  (She sees Prior crying. She glares at Harper)
  What did you do to him?

HARPER: Nothing! He just can't *adjust*, is all, he just . . .

(Hannah has gone to the diorama. She yanks the curtain open.)

HARPER: NO WAIT. Don't . . .

(The father dummy is back—a real dummy this time.)

HARPER: Oh. *(To Prior)* Look, we . . . imagined it.

HANNAH: This is a favor, they let me work here as a favor, but you keep making scenes, and look at this mess, it's a garbage scow!

HARPER *(Over Hannah, to Prior)*: It doesn't look so much like him, now. He's changed. Again.

HANNAH *(Overlapping)*: Are you just going to sit here forever, trash piling higher, day after day till. . . . Well till what?

HARPER *(Overlapping)*: You sound just like him. You even grind your teeth in your sleep like him.

HANNAH *(Overlapping)*: If I could get him to come back I would go back to Salt Lake tomorrow but I know my duty when I see it, and if you and Joe could say the same we . . .

HARPER *(Overlapping)*: You can't go back to Salt Lake, you sold your house! *(To Prior)* My mother-in-law! She sold her house! Her son calls and tells her he's a homo and what does she do? She sells her house! And she calls *me* crazy! You have less of a place in this world than *I* do if that's possible.

PRIOR: Am I dreaming this, I don't understand.

HARPER: He saw an angel.

HANNAH: That's his business.

HARPER: He's an angelologist.

PRIOR: Well don't go blabbing about it.

HANNAH *(To Prior)*: If you aren't serious you shouldn't come in here.

HARPER *(Simultaneously)*: Either that or he's nuts.

PRIOR: It's a visitor's center; I'm visiting.

HARPER: He has a point.

HANNAH *(To Harper)*: Quiet!
　　　(To Prior) It's for serious visitors, it's a serious religion.

PRIOR: Do they like, *pay* you to do this?

HARPER: She volunteers.

PRIOR: Because you're not very hospitable. I did see an angel.

HANNAH: And what do you want me to do about it? I have problems of my own.
　　　The diorama's closed for repairs. You have to leave.
　　　(To Harper) Clean up this mess. *(Exits)*

(Harper and Prior look at each other.)

HARPER *(Pointing to the Mormon Mother)*: His wife. His mute wife. I'm waiting for her to speak. Bet her story's not so jolly.

PRIOR: Imagination is a dangerous thing.

HARPER *(Looking at the father dummy)*: In certain circumstances, fatal. It can blow up in your face. If it turns out to be true. Threshold . . .

PRIOR AND HARPER: . . . of revelation.

(They look at each other.)

PRIOR: It's crazy time. I feel . . . this is nuts. I feel . . . this is nuts. We've never met, but I feel you know me incredibly well.

HARPER: Crazy time. The barn door's open now, and all the cows have fled.

You don't look well. You really should be home in bed.

PRIOR: I'll die there.

HARPER: Better in bed than on the street. Just ask anyone.

Till we meet again.

(Prior leaves. Harper sits alone for a moment, then:)

HARPER: Bitter lady of the Plains, talk to me. Tell me what to do.

(The Mormon Mother turns to Harper, then stands and leaves the diorama stage. She gestures with her head for Harper to follow her.)

HARPER: I'm stuck. My heart's an anchor.

MORMON MOTHER: Leave it, then. Can't carry no extra weight.

(The Mormon Mother leaves the diorama. Harper sits a moment. She goes to the diorama, gets in the Mormon Mother's seat.)

HARPER *(To the dummy father)*: Look at us. So perfect in place. The desert the mountains the previous century. Maybe I could have believed in you then. Maybe we should never have moved east.

MORMON MOTHER: Come on.

(They exit.)

Scene 4

Late that afternoon. Joe and Louis sitting shoulder to shoulder in the dunes at Jones Beach, facing the ocean. It's cold. The sound of waves and gulls and distant Belt Parkway traffic. New York Romantic. Joe is very cold, Louis as always is oblivious to the weather.

LOUIS: The winter Atlantic. Wow, huh?
    There used to be guys in the dunes even when it snowed. Nothing deterred us from the task at hand.

JOE: Which was?

LOUIS: Exploration. Across an unmapped terrain. The body of the homosexual human male. Here, or the Ramble, or the scrub pines on Fire Island, or the St. Mark's Baths. Hardy pioneers. Like your ancestors.

JOE: Not exactly.

LOUIS: And many have perished on the trail.
    I fucked around a lot more than he did. No justice.

(Little pause.)

JOE: I love it when you can get to places and see what it used
    to be. The whole country was like this once. A paradise.

LOUIS: Ruined now.

JOE: It's still a great country. Best place on earth. Best place to
    be.

LOUIS *(Staring at him a beat, then)*: OY. A *Mormon.*

JOE: You never asked.

LOUIS: So what else haven't you told me?

    Joe?

    So the fruity underwear you wear, that's . . .

JOE: A temple garment.

LOUIS: *Oh my God.* What's it for?

JOE: Protection. A second skin. I can stop wearing it if you . . .

LOUIS: How can you stop wearing it if it's a skin? Your past,
    your beliefs, your . . .

(Joe tousles Louis's hair. Louis pulls away.)

JOE: I know how you feel, I keep expecting divine retribution
    for this, but. . . . I'm actually happy. Actually.

LOUIS: You're not happy, no one is happy. What am I doing?
    With you? With *anyone*, I should be exterminated but
    with *you*: married probably bisexual Mormon Republican
    closet case. I mean I really *like* you a lot but . . .

(Joe puts his hand over Louis's mouth.)

JOE: Shut up, OK?

*(Louis nods. Joe takes his hand off Louis's mouth and kisses
him, deeply.)*

JOE: You believe the world is perfectible and so you find it always unsatisfying.

(Joe kisses Louis again, begins to unbutton Louis's shirt.)

JOE: You have to reconcile yourself to the world's unper-fectibility by being thoroughly *in* the world but not *of* it.

(Joe bites Louis's nipple.)

LOUIS: Oh God . . .
JOE: That's what being a Mormon is.
LOUIS: That's what being a schizophrenic is.

(Joe looks over his shoulder to see that no one is watching, then he hauls Louis onto his lap, unzips Louis's fly and slides his hand inside Louis's pants. Louis moans.)

JOE: The rhythm of history is conservative. You have to accept that. And accept as rightfully yours the happiness that comes your way.
LOUIS: But. . . . Wait. Oh God. But the Republican party. . . . Mmmmmmm . . . is. . . . I mean. . . . Newt Gingrich, Jesse Helms. . . . I hate the Democrats too but the Republicans . . .
JOE: Responsible for everything bad and evil in the world.
LOUIS: Throw Reagan on the pile and you're not far off.
JOE: Oh if people like you didn't have President Reagan to demonize where would you be?
LOUIS: If he didn't have people like me to demonize where would *he* be? Upper-right-hand square on *The Hollywood Squares.*

(Louis kisses Joe, very turned-on.)

LOUIS: This is interesting. I'm losing myself in an ideological leather bar. The more appalling I find your politics the more I want to hump you.

JOE: I'm not your enemy. Louis.

LOUIS: I never said you were my . . .

JOE: Fundamentally, we both want the same thing.

(They look at each other. Louis disentangles himself a little, gently.)

LOUIS: I don't think that's true.

JOE: It is.

What you did when you walked out on him was hard to do. The world may not understand it or approve but you did what you needed to do. And I consider you very brave.

LOUIS: Nobody does what I did, Joe. Nobody.

JOE: But maybe many want to.

Let him go. For real. Louis.

I love you.

LOUIS: No you don't.

JOE: Yes I do.

LOUIS: NO YOU DON'T. You can't, it's only been a month, it takes years to fall in love, four-and-a-half years minimum. You *think* you do but that's just the gay virgin thing, that's . . .

JOE: You and I, Louis, we are the same. We both want the same thing.

LOUIS: I want to see Prior again.

(Joe stands up, moves away.)

LOUIS: I miss him, I . . .

JOE: You want to go back to . . .

LOUIS: I just. . . . Need to see him again.

Don't you. . . . You must want to see your wife.

JOE: I miss her, I feel bad for her, I. . . . I'm afraid of her.

LOUIS: Yes.

JOE: And I want more to be with . . .

LOUIS: I have to. See him.

It's been a month, I'm worried. I just.

Please don't look so sad.

Do you understand what I . . .

JOE: You don't want to see me anymore.

LOUIS *(Uncertainly)*: No, I . . .

JOE: Louis.

Anything.

LOUIS: What?

JOE: Anything. Whatever you want. I can give up anything. My skin.

(Joe starts to remove his clothes. Louis, when he realizes what Joe is doing, tries to stop him.)

LOUIS: What are you doing, someone will see us, it's not a nude beach, it's freezing!

(Joe pushes Louis away, Louis falls, and Joe removes most of the rest of his clothing, tearing the temple garment off. He's almost naked.)

JOE: I'm flayed. No past now. I could give up anything. Maybe . . . in what we've been doing, maybe I'm even infected.

LOUIS: No you're . . .

JOE: I don't want to be. I want to live now. And I can be anything I need to be. And I want to be with you.

(Louis starts to dress Joe.)

JOE: You have a good heart and you think the good thing is to be guilty and kind always but it's not always kind to be gentle and soft, there's a genuine violence softness and weakness visit on people. Sometimes self-interested is the most generous thing you can be.

You ought to think about that.

LOUIS: I will. Think about it.

JOE: You ought to think about . . . what you're doing to me. No, I mean. . . . What you need. Think about what you need. Be brave.

(Louis starts to walk away from Joe. Joe calls after him:)

JOE: And then you'll come back to me.

(Louis stands, facing away from Joe. Joe calls loudly, furiously.)

JOE: AND THEN YOU'LL COME BACK TO ME!

Scene 5

Night of the same day. Louis and Joe remain onstage from previous scene.

Roy's hospital room. Roy is asleep. Belize enters, carrying a tray and a glass of water. He wakes Roy up.

BELIZE: Time to take your pills.

ROY *(Waking)*: What? What time of . . .

Water.

(Belize gives him a glass of water.)

ROY: Bitter.

Look out there. Black midnight.

BELIZE: You want anything?

ROY: Nothing that comes from there. As far as I'm concerned
you can take all that away.

(Seeing Belize) Oh . . .

BELIZE: What?

ROY *(Putting his hands down)*: Oh. The bogeyman is here.

Lookit, Ma, a schvartze toytenmann.

Come in, sweetheart, what took you so long?

BELIZE: You're flying, Roy. It's the morphine. They put morphine in the drip to stop the. . . . You awake? Can you see
who I am?

ROY: Oh yeah, you came for my mama, years ago.

You wrap your arms around me now. Squeeze the
bloody life from me. OK?

BELIZE: Uh, no, it's not OK. You're stoned, Roy.

ROY: Dark strong arms, take me like that. Deep and sincere
but not too rough, just open me up to the end of me.

BELIZE: Who am I, Roy?

ROY: The Negro night nurse, my negation. You've come to
escort me to the underworld. *(A serious sexual invitation)*
Come on.

BELIZE: You want me in your bed, Roy? You want me to take
you away.

ROY: I'm ready . . .

BELIZE: I'll be coming for you soon. Everything I want is in the end of you.

(Belize starts to move away from Roy.)

ROY: Let me ask you something, sir.
BELIZE: *Sir?*
ROY: What's it like? After?
BELIZE: After . . . ?
ROY: This misery ends.
BELIZE: Hell or heaven?

(Roy stares at Belize, as in "What a stupid question.")

BELIZE: Like San Francisco.
ROY: A city. Good. I was worried . . . it'd be a garden. I hate that shit.
BELIZE: Mmmm.

Big city, overgrown with weeds, but flowering weeds. On every corner a wrecking crew and something new and crooked going up catty-corner to that. Windows missing in every edifice like broken teeth, fierce gusts of gritty wind, and a gray high sky full of ravens.
ROY: Isaiah.
BELIZE: Prophet birds, Roy.

Piles of trash, but lapidary like rubies and obsidian, and diamond-colored cowspit streamers in the wind. And voting booths.
ROY: And a dragon atop a golden horde.
BELIZE: And everyone in Balenciaga gowns with red corsages, and big dance palaces full of music and lights and racial impurity and gender confusion.

(Roy laughs softly, delighted.)

BELIZE: And all the deities are creole, mulatto, brown as the mouths of rivers.

(Roy laughs again.)

BELIZE: Race, taste and history finally overcome.
        And you ain't there.
ROY *(Happily shaking his head "no" in agreement)*: And Heaven?
BELIZE: That *was* Heaven, Roy.
ROY: The fuck it was.
        (Suspicious, frightened) Who are you?

(Little pause.)

BELIZE *(Whispering)*: Your negation.
ROY: Yeah. I know you. Nothing. A stomach grumble that wakes you in the night.

(Ethel enters.)

BELIZE: Been nice talking to you. Go to sleep now, baby. I'm just the shadow on your grave.

Scene 6

Harper and the Mormon Mother. Night. At the Brooklyn Heights Promenade. Everyone from the previous two scenes remains onstage.

HARPER: It's not safe to be out on the street here, there are crazy people around.

MORMON MOTHER *(Looking at the skyline)*: Towers filled with fire. It's the Great Beyond.

HARPER: Manhattan. Was it a hard thing, crossing the prairies?

MORMON MOTHER: You ain't stupid. So don't ask stupid. Ask something for real.

HARPER *(A beat, then)*: In your experience of the world. How do people change?

MORMON MOTHER: Well it has something to do with God so it's not very nice.

God splits the skin with a jagged thumbnail from throat to belly and then plunges a huge filthy hand in, he grabs hold of your bloody tubes and they slip to evade his grasp but he squeezes hard, he *insists*, he pulls and pulls till all your innards are yanked out and the pain! We can't even talk about that. And then he stuffs them back, dirty, tangled and torn. It's up to you to do the stitching.

HARPER: And then get up. And walk around.

MORMON MOTHER: Just mangled guts pretending.

HARPER: That's how people change.

(Prior appears. He's at home, slowly unwrapping his layers of black prophet clothes. He is very sick and sad.)

MORMON MOTHER: I smell a salt wind.

HARPER: From the ocean.

MORMON MOTHER: Means he's coming back. Then you'll know. Then you'll eat fire.
(Singing)
Bring back, bring back,
Oh bring back my bonnie to me, to me . . .

HARPER *(Joining in)*:
>Bring back, bring back,
>Oh bring back my bonnie to me.

(As they sing, Louis leaves Joe alone at the beach. Back in Manhattan, he goes to a street-side payphone, dials a number. Prior is alone in his bedroom. He is taking his medication. The phone rings in Prior's apartment. Prior picks it up.)

PRIOR: Wait, I have a mouthful of pills and water, I . . .
LOUIS: Prior? It's Lou.

(Prior swallows.)

LOUIS: I want to see you.

ACT FOUR:

John Brown's Body

February 1986

Scene 1

A day later. Split scene: Louis sitting, cold, on a park bench. Roy and Joe in Roy's hospital room. Roy's in bed, hooked up as usual to an IV drip. His condition has worsened. Joe sits in a chair nearby.

ROY: If you want the smoke and puffery you can listen to Kissinger and Schultz and those guys, but if you want to look at the heart of modern conservatism, you look at me. Everyone else has abandoned the struggle, everything nowadays is just sipping tea with Nixon and Mao, that was *disgusting*, did you see that? Were you born yet?

JOE: Of course I . . .

ROY: My generation, we had *clarity*. Unafraid to look deep into the miasma at the heart of the world, what a pit, what a nightmare is there—*I* have looked, I have searched all my life for absolute bottom, and I found it, *believe* me:

Stygian. How tragic, how brutal and short life is. How sinful people are. The immutable heart of what we are that bleeds through whatever we might become. All else is vanity.

I don't know the world anymore.

(He coughs)

After I die they'll say it was for the money and the headlines. But it was never the money: It's the moxie that counts. I never wavered. You: remember.

JOE: I will, Roy.

I was afraid you wouldn't want to see me. If you'd forgive me. For letting you down.

ROY: Forgiveness. You seen a lady around here, dumpy lady, stupid . . . hat? She. . . . Oh boy. Oh boy, no she's off watching the hearings. Treacherous bitch.

JOE: Who?

ROY: Did you get a blessing from your father before he died?

JOE: A blessing?

ROY: Yeah.

JOE: No.

ROY: He should have done that. Life. That's what they're supposed to bless. Life.

(Roy motions for Joe to come over, then for him to kneel. He puts his hand on Joe's forehead. Joe leans the weight of his head into Roy's hand. They both close their eyes and enjoy it for a moment.)

JOE *(Quietly)*: Roy, I. . . . I need to talk to you about . . .

ROY: Ssshah. Schmendrick. Don't fuck up the magic.

(He removes his hand) A *Brokhe.* You don't even have to trick it out of me, like what's-his-name in the Bible.

JOE: Jacob.

ROY: That's the one. A ruthless motherfucker, some bald runt, but he laid hold of his birthright with his claws and his teeth. Jacob's father—what was the guy's name?

JOE: Isaac.

ROY: Yeah. The sacrifice. That jerk.

My mother read me those stories.

See this scar on my nose? When I was three months old, there was a bony spur, she made them operate, shave it off. They said I was too young for surgery, I'd outgrow it but she insisted. I figure she wanted to toughen me up. And it worked.

I am tough. It's taking a lot . . . to dismantle me.

(Prior enters and sits on the bench, as far as he can from Lou.)

PRIOR: Oh this is going to be so much worse than I'd imagined.

LOUIS: Hello.

PRIOR: Fuck you you little shitbag.

LOUIS: Don't waste energy beating up on me, OK? I'm already taking care of that.

PRIOR: Don't see any bruises.

LOUIS: Inside.

PRIOR: You are one noble guy. Inside. Don't flatter yourself, Louis.

So. It's your tea party. Talk.

LOUIS: It's good to see you again. I missed you.

PRIOR: Talk.

LOUIS: I want to . . . try to make up.

PRIOR: Make up.

LOUIS: Yes. But . . .

PRIOR: Aha. But.

LOUIS: But you don't have to be so hostile. Don't I get any points for trying to arrive at a resolution? Maybe what I did isn't forgivable but . . .

PRIOR: It isn't.

LOUIS: But. I'm trying to be responsible. Prior. There are limits. Boundaries. And you have to be reasonable.

Why are you dressed like that?

(Little pause.)

PRIOR: You were saying something about being reasonable.

LOUIS: I've been giving this a lot of thought. Yes I fucked up, that's obvious. But maybe you fucked up too. You never trusted me, you never gave me a chance to find my footing, not really, you were so quick to attack and. . . . I think, maybe just too much of a victim, finally. Passive. Dependent. And what I think is that people do have a choice about how they handle . . .

PRIOR: You want to come back. Why? Atonement? Exoneration?

LOUIS: I didn't say I wanted to come back.

(Pause.)

PRIOR: Oh.

No, you didn't.

LOUIS *(Softly, almost pleading)*: I can't. Move in again, start all over again. I don't think it'd be any different.

(Little pause.)

PRIOR: You're seeing someone else.

LOUIS *(Shocked)*: What? No.

PRIOR: You are.

LOUIS: I'M NOT. Well, occasionally a . . . he's a . . . just a pickup, how do you . . .

PRIOR: Threshold of revelation. Now: Ask me how I know he's a Mormon.

(Pause. Louis stares.)

PRIOR: *Is* he a Mormon?

> *(Little pause)*
> Well, goddamn. Ask me how I knew.

LOUIS: How?

PRIOR: Fuck you. I'm a prophet.

> *(Furious) Reasonable? Limits?* Tell it to my *lungs*, stupid, tell it to my lesions, tell it to the cotton-woolly patches in my eyes!

LOUIS: Prior, I . . . haven't seen him for days now . . .

PRIOR: I'm going, I have limits too.

(Prior starts to leave. He has an attack of some sort of respiratory trouble. He sits heavily on the bench. Louis starts to go near him, Prior waves him away. Prior looks at Louis.)

PRIOR: You cry, but you endanger nothing in yourself. It's like the idea of crying when you do it.

> Or the idea of love.

ROY: Now you have to go.

JOE: I left my wife.

> *(Little pause)*
> I needed to tell you.

ROY: It happens.

JOE: I've been staying with someone. Else. For a whole month now.

ROY: It happens.

JOE: With a man.

(Pause.)

ROY: A man?
JOE: Yes.
ROY: You're with a man?
JOE: Yes I . . .

(Roy sits up in his bed. He puts his legs over the side, away from where Joe is sitting.)

ROY: I gotta . . .
JOE: You . . . what, the . . . um, bathroom or . . .

(Roy stands, unsteadily. He starts to walk away from the bed. The IV tube in his arm extends to its full length and then pulls. Roy looks down at it, remembering it's there. In a calm, disinterested manner he pulls it out of his arm, which starts bleeding profusely.)

ROY: Ow.
JOE: Roy, what are you . . .

(Joe starts for the door, Roy stands still watching dark blood run down his arm.)

JOE *(Calling off)*: Um, help, please, I think he . . .

(Belize enters with the portable oxygen, and then sees Roy.)

BELIZE: Holy shit.

(Belize puts on rubber gloves, starts towards Roy.)

ROY: Get the fuck away from me.
JOE *(Going towards Roy)*: Roy, please, get back into . . .
ROY: SHUT UP!
  Now you listen to me.

(Joe nods.)

BELIZE: Get your . . .
ROY: SHUT UP I SAID.
  (To Joe) I want you home. With your wife. Whatever else you got going, cut it dead.
JOE: I can't, Roy, I need to be with . . .

(Roy grabs Joe by the shirt, smearing it with blood.)

ROY: YOU NEED? Listen to me. Do what I say. Or you will regret it.
  And don't talk to me about it. *Ever again.*

(Belize moves in, takes Roy to the bed and starts bandaging the puncture.)

ROY: I . . . never saw that coming. You kill me.
BELIZE *(To Joe)*: Get somewhere you can take off that shirt and throw it out, and don't touch the blood.
JOE: Why? I don't unders . . .
ROY: OUT! OUT! You already got my blessing—WHAT MORE DO YOU WANT FROM ME?

(He has a terrible wracking spasm.)

BELIZE *(To Joe)*: Get the fuck outta here.

JOE: I. . . . Roy, please I . . .

ROY *(Exhausted)*: You what, you want to stay and watch *this*? Well fuck you too.

(Joe leaves. Belize finishes bandaging.)

PRIOR: So. Your new lover . . .

LOUIS: He's not my . . .

PRIOR: Tell me where you met him.

LOUIS: In the park. Well, first at work, he . . .

PRIOR: He's a lawyer or a judge?

LOUIS: Lawyer.

PRIOR: A Gay Mormon Lawyer.

LOUIS: Yes. Republican too.

PRIOR: A Gay Mormon Republican Lawyer. *(With contempt)* Louis . . .

LOUIS: But he's sort of, I don't know if the word would be . . . well, in a way sensitive, and I . . .

PRIOR: Ah. A *sensitive* gay Republican.

LOUIS: He's just company. Companionship.

(Pause.)

PRIOR: Companionship. Oh.

You know just when I think he couldn't possibly say anything to make it worse, he does. Companionship. How *good*. I wouldn't want you to be *lonely*.

There are thousands of gay men in New York City with AIDS and nearly every one of them is being taken care of by . . . a friend or by . . . a lover who has stuck by them through things worse than my. . . . So far. Everyone got that, except me. I got you. Why? What's wrong with me?

(Louis is crying)

PRIOR: Louis?

Are you really bruised inside?

LOUIS: I can't have this talk anymore.

PRIOR: Oh the list of things you can't do. So fragile! Answer me: Inside: Bruises?

LOUIS: Yes.

PRIOR: Come back to me when they're visible. I want to see black and blue, Louis, I want to see blood. Because I can't believe you even *have* blood in your veins till you show it to me. So don't come near me again, unless you've got something to show. *(Exits)*

ROY *(Looking at the door through which Joe exited)*: Every goddam thing I ever wanted they have taken from me. Mocked and reviled, all my life.

BELIZE: Join the club.

ROY: I don't belong to any club you could get through the front door of. You watch yourself you take too many liberties.

What's your name?

BELIZE *(A beat, then)*: Norman Arriaga. Belize to my friends, but you can call me Norman Arriaga.

ROY: Tell me something, Norman, you ever hire a lawyer?

BELIZE: No Roy. Never did.

ROY: Hire a lawyer, sue somebody, it's good for the soul.

Lawyers are . . . the High Priests of America. We alone know the words that made America. Out of thin air. We alone know how to use The Words. The Law: the only club I ever wanted to belong to. And before they take that from me, I'm going to die.

(Roy has a series of terrible spasms, which shake him violently. Belize approaches. Roy grabs Belize by both arms. Belize tries to pull away, but Roy hangs on, shaking them both. During this seizure, Ethel appears.)

ROY: Sssshhh. Fire. Out. *(It isn't. Violent spasms continue)*
    God have mercy. This is a lousy way to go.

BELIZE: God have mercy.

ROY *(Seeing Ethel)*: Look who's back.

BELIZE *(Looking around, seeing no one)*: Who?

ROY: Mrs. Reddy Kilowatt.
    Fucking horror. How's. . . . Yonkers?

BELIZE: I almost feel sorry for you.

ETHEL: A bad idea.

ROY: Yeah. Pity. Repulsive.
    (To Belize) You. Me. *(He snaps his fingers)* No. Connection.
    Nobody . . . with me now. But the dead.

Scene 2

The next day. Joe in his office at the courthouse in Brooklyn. He sits at his desk dejectedly, head in hands. Prior and Belize enter the corridor outside.

PRIOR *(Whisper)*: That's his office.

BELIZE *(Whisper)*: This is stupid.

PRIOR *(Whisper)*: Go home if you're chicken.

BELIZE: *You're* the one who should be home.

PRIOR: I have a hobby now: haunting people. Fuck home. You
    wait here. I want to meet my replacement.

(Prior goes to Joe's door, steps in.)

PRIOR: Oh.

JOE: Yes, can I . . .

PRIOR: You look just like the dummy. She's right.

JOE: Who's right?

PRIOR: Your wife.

(Pause.)

JOE: What?

Do you know my . . .

PRIOR: No.

JOE: You said my wife.

PRIOR: No I didn't.

JOE: Yes you did.

PRIOR: You misheard. I'm a Prophet.

JOE: What?

PRIOR: PROPHET PROPHET I PROPHESY I HAVE SIGHT I *SEE*.

What do *you* do?

JOE: I'm a clerk.

PRIOR: Oh big deal. A clerk. You *what*, you file things? Well you better be keeping a file on the hearts you break, that's all that counts in the end, you'll have bills to pay in the world to come, you and your friend, the Whore of Babylon.

(Pause)

Sorry wrong room.

(Prior exits, goes to Belize.)

PRIOR *(Despairing)*: He's the Marlboro Man.

BELIZE: Oooh, I wanna see.

(Belize goes to Joe's office. Joe is standing, perplexed. Belize sees Joe and instantly recognizes him.)

BELIZE: *SACRED* Heart of Jesus!

JOE: Now what is . . .

    You're Roy's nurse. I recognize you, you're . . .

BELIZE: No you don't.

JOE: From the hospital. You're Roy Cohn's nurse.

BELIZE: No I'm not. Not a nurse. We all look alike to you. You all look alike to us. It's a mad mad world. Have a nice day.

    (Exits, back to Prior)

PRIOR: Home on the range?

BELIZE: Chaps and spurs. Now girl we *got* to get you home and into . . .

PRIOR: Mega-butch. He made me feel beyond nelly. Like little wispy daisies were sprouting out my ears. Little droopy wispy wilted . . .

    (Joe comes out of his office.)

BELIZE: Run! Run!

JOE: Wait!

    (They're cornered by Joe. Belize keeps his face averted and covered.)

JOE: What game are you playing, this is a federal courthouse. You said . . . something about my wife. Now what. . . . How do you know my . . .

PRIOR: I'm. . . . Nothing. I'm a mental patient. He's my nurse.

BELIZE: Not his nurse, I'm not a n . . .

PRIOR: We're here because my will is being contested. Um, what is that called, when they challenge your will?

JOE: Competency? But this is an appellate court.

PRIOR: And I am appealing to anyone, anyone in the universe, who will listen to me for some. . . . Charity. . . . Some people are so greedy, such pigs, they have everything, health, everything, and still they want more.

JOE: You said my wife. And I want to know, is she . . .

PRIOR: TALK TO HER YOURSELF, BULLWINKLE! WHAT DO I LOOK LIKE A MARRIAGE COUNSELOR?

Oh nursey dear, fetch the medication, I'm starting to rave.

BELIZE: Pardons, Monsieur l' Avocat, nous sommes absolument Desolée.

(Prior blows a raspberry at Joe.)

BELIZE: Behave yourself, cherie, or nanny will have to use the wooden spoon.

(Prior exits.)

BELIZE *(To Joe, dropping scarf disguise)*: I am trapped in a world of white people. That's *my* problem. *(Exits)*

Scene 3

The next day, a stormy cold late-February day. At the Bethesda Fountain in Central Park. As the scene progresses a storm front moves in and the day darkens. Louis is sitting on the fountain's rim. Belize enters and sits next to him.

BELIZE: Nice angel.
LOUIS: What angel?
BELIZE: The fountain.

LOUIS *(Looking)*: Bethesda.

BELIZE: What's she commemorate? Louis, I'll bet you know.

LOUIS: Naval dead of the Civil War.

BELIZE: The Civil War. I knew you'd know. You are nothing if not well informed.

LOUIS: Listen. I saw Prior yesterday.

BELIZE: Prior is *upset*.

LOUIS: Listen, this guy I'm seeing, I'm not seeing him now. Prior misunderstood, he jumped to . . .

BELIZE: Oh yeah. Your new beau. Prior and me, we went to the courthouse. Scoped him out.

LOUIS: *You had no right to do that.*

BELIZE: Oh did we violate your *rights*. What did you drag me out here for, Louis, I don't have *time* for you. You walk out on your lover. Days don't pass before you are out on the town with somebody new. But *this* . . .

LOUIS: I'm *not* out on the. . . . I want you to tell Prior that I . . .

BELIZE: *This* is a record low: sharing your dank and dirty bed with Roy Cohn's buttboy.

(Pause.)

LOUIS: Come again?

BELIZE: Doesn't that bother you at all?

LOUIS: *Roy Cohn?* What the fuck are you. . . . I am not sharing my bed with Roy Cohn's . . .

BELIZE: Your little friend didn't tell you, huh? You and Hoss Cartwright, it's not a verbal kind of thing, you just kick off your boots and hit the hay.

LOUIS: Joe Pitt is not Roy Cohn's. . . . Joe is a very moral man, he's not even *that* conservative, or . . . well not that *kind* of a. . . . And I don't want to continue this.

BELIZE *(Starting to go)*: Bye-bye.

LOUIS: It's not my fault that Prior left you for me.

BELIZE: I beg your pardon.

LOUIS: You have always hated me. Because you are in love with Prior and you were when I met him and he fell in love with me, and so now you cook up this. . . . I mean how do you know this? That Joe and *Roy Cohn* are . . .

BELIZE: I don't know whether Mr. Cohn has penetrated more than his spiritual sphincter. All I'm saying is you better hope there's no GOP germ, Louis, 'cause if there is, you got it.

LOUIS: *I don't believe you.* Not *Roy Cohn.* He's like the polestar of human evil, he's like the worst human being who ever lived, he isn't *human* even, he's. . . . Give me credit for *something*, please, some little moral shred of, of, of *something*, OK sure I fucked up, I fucked everything up, I fucked up everything maybe more than anyone in the whole history of everything that's ever been ever fucked up but still I haven't. . . . I haven't lost my mind, I'm not *insane*, I'm. . . . I'm horribly horribly unhappy, I'm lost, I'm. . . . I hate myself, so totally, so fucking totally and completely but still I wouldn't, I wouldn't go around sleeping with someone who . . . someone who's *Roy Cohn's* . . .

   (He stops himself)

BELIZE: Buttboy.

LOUIS *(In complete despair, quietly)*: Oh God. I am so fucking wet and miserable.

BELIZE: You know what your problem is, Louis? Your problem is that you are so full of piping hot crap that the mention of your name draws flies. You don't even know Thing One about this guy, do you?

(Louis shakes his head "no.")

BELIZE: Uh huh. Well ain't that pathetic.

Just so's the record's straight: I love Prior but I was never in love with him. I have a man, uptown, and I have since *long* before I first laid my eyes on the sorry-ass sight of you.

LOUIS: I. . . . I didn't know that you . . .

BELIZE: No 'cause you never bothered to ask.

Up in the air, just like that angel, too far off the earth to pick out the details. Louis and his Big Ideas. Big Ideas are all you love. "America" is what Louis loves.

(Little pause.)

LOUIS: So what? Maybe I do. You don't know what I love. You don't.

BELIZE: Well I hate America, Louis. I hate this country. It's just big ideas, and stories, and people dying, and people like you.

The white cracker who wrote the national anthem knew what he was doing. He set the word "free" to a note so high nobody can reach it. That was deliberate. Nothing on earth sounds less like freedom to me.

You come with me to room 1013 over at the hospital, I'll show you America. Terminal, crazy and mean.

(A rumble of thunder. Then the rain comes. Belize has a collapsible umbrella, and he raises it. Louis stands in the rain.)

BELIZE: I *live* in America, Louis, that's hard enough, I don't have to love it. You do that. Everybody's got to love something.

LOUIS: Everybody does.

Scene 4

Same day. Hannah at the Visitor's Center. Joe enters. They look at each other for a long moment.

JOE: How is she?

HANNAH: Nothing surprising.

JOE: Is she OK?

HANNAH: Well *that* would be surprising. Wouldn't it?
 Can I . . .

JOE: There is no possible thing I can imagine you doing. Ma. You shouldn't have come.

HANNAH: You already made that clear as day. For a month now. You can't even return a simple phone call.

JOE: A phone call from you . . . is not so simple.

HANNAH: Just so I would have something to tell her. You've been living on some rainy rooftop for all we knew. It's cruel.

JOE: Not intended to be.

HANNAH: You're sure about that.

JOE *(A beat, then)*: I'm taking her home.

HANNAH: You think that's best for her, you think that she . . .

JOE: I know what I'm doing.

HANNAH: I don't think you have a clue. Which is only typical of you. You're a man, you botch up, it's not such a big deal, but she . . .

JOE: Just being a man doesn't . . .

HANNAH: Being a woman's harder. Look at her.

JOE *(A beat, then, softly)*: It's a big deal, Ma, botching up. I could use some . . .

HANNAH: Sympathy?
 (Little pause)

If I could manage any, you'd just push it away. You want sympathy? Then why'd you come here?

JOE: I migrated across the breadth of the continent of North America, I ran all this way to get away from . . . *(He stops)* Is she . . . ?

HANNAH: She's not here.

JOE: But . . . she's not at the apartment, I . . .

HANNAH *(A beat, then)*: Then she escaped. Good for her.
    Ask yourself what it was you were running from. It's time you did. Not from me, I was nothing. From what? And what are you running from now?

JOE: You and me. It's like we're back in Salt Lake again. You sort of bring the desert with you.
    (Little pause)
    Are you. . . . Don't cry.

HANNAH: If I ever do. I promise you you'll not be privileged to witness it.

JOE: It was a mistake. I should never have called you. Ma. You should never have come. I can't imagine why you did.

*(Joe exits. Hannah sits.
    Prior enters, wearing dark glasses and a hat.)*

PRIOR: That man who was just here.

HANNAH *(Not looking at him)*: We're closed. Go away.

PRIOR: He's your son.

(Hannah looks at Prior. Little pause. Prior turns to leave.)

HANNAH: Do you know him. That man?
    (Little pause)
    How do you know that . . .

PRIOR: My ex-boyfriend, he knows him, *now*—I wanted to warn your son about *later*, when his hair goes and there's hips and jowls and all that . . . human stuff, that poor slob there's just gonna wind up miserable, fat, frightened and *alone* because Louis, he can't handle bodies.

HANNAH *(A beat, then)*: Are you a . . . a homosexual?

PRIOR: Oh is it *that* obvious? Yes. I am. What's it to you?

HANNAH: Would you say you are a typical . . . homosexual?

PRIOR: Me? Oh I'm *stereotypical*. What, you mean like am I a hairdresser or . . .

HANNAH: Are you a hairdresser?

PRIOR: Well it would be *your* lucky day if I was because frankly . . .

> I'm sick. I'm sick. It's expensive.
> *(He starts to cry)*
> Oh shit now I won't be able to stop, now it's started. I feel really terrible, do I have a fever? *(Offering his forehead, impatiently)*
> Do I have a fever?

(She hesitates, then puts her hand on his forehead.)

HANNAH: Yes.

PRIOR: How high?

HANNAH: There might be a thermometer in the . . .

PRIOR: Very high, very high, could you get me to a cab, I think I want . . . *(He sits heavily on the floor)* Don't be alarmed, it's worse than it looks, I mean . . .

HANNAH: You should. . . . Try to stand up, or . . . let me see if anyone can . . .

PRIOR *(Listening to his lungs)*: Sssshhh.
> Echo-breath, it's . . . *(He shakes his head "no good")* I . . . overdid it. I'm in trouble again.

Take me to St. Vincent's Hospital, I mean, help me to a cab to the . . .

(Little pause, then Hannah exits and reenters with her coat on.)

HANNAH: Can you stand up?
PRIOR: You don't. . . . Call me a . . .
HANNAH: I'm useless here.

(She helps him stand.)

PRIOR: Please, if you're trying to convert me this isn't a good time.

(Distant thunder.)

HANNAH: Lord, look at it out there. It's pitch-black. Storm's coming in. We better move.

(They exit. Thunder.)

Scene 5

Same day, late afternoon. Harper is standing in an icy March wind at the railing of the Promenade in Brooklyn Heights, staring at the river and the Manhattan skyline. The rain is starting. She is wearing a dress, inadequate for the weather, and she's barefoot. Joe enters with an umbrella. They stare at each other. Then Harper turns to face the skyline.

HARPER: The end of the world is at hand. Hello, paleface.

Nothing like storm clouds over Manhattan to get you in the mood for Judgment Day.

(Thunder.)

JOE: It's freezing, it's starting to rain, where are your shoes?

HARPER: I threw them in the river.

The Judgment Day. Everyone will think they're crazy now, not just me, everyone will see things. Sick men will see angels, women who have houses will sell their houses, dimestore dummies will rear up on their wood-putty legs and roam the land, looking for brides.

JOE: Let's go home.

HARPER: Where's that?

(Pointing towards Manhattan) Want to buy an island? It's going out of business. You can have it for the usual cheap trinkets. Fire sale. The prices are insane.

JOE: Harper.

HARPER: Joe. Did you miss me?

JOE: I. . . . I've come back.

HARPER: Oh I know.

Here's why I wanted to stay in Brooklyn. The Promenade view.

Water won't ever accomplish the end. No matter how much you cry. Flood's not the answer, people just float.

Let's go home.

Fire's the answer. The Great and Terrible Day. At last.

Scene 6

Night. Prior, Emily (Prior's nurse-practitioner) and Hannah in an examination room in St. Vincent's emergency room. Emily is listening to his breathing, while Hannah sits in a nearby chair.

EMILY: You've lost eight pounds. Eight pounds! I know people who would kill to be in the shape you were in, you were *recovering*, and you threw it away.

PRIOR: This isn't about WEIGHT, it's about LUNGS, UM . . . PNEUMONIA.

EMILY: We don't know yet.

PRIOR: THE FUCK WE DON'T ASSHOLE YOU MAY NOT BUT I *CAN'T BREATHE*.

HANNAH: You'd breathe better if you didn't holler like that.

PRIOR *(Looks at Hannah, then)*: This is my ex-lover's lover's Mormon mother.

(Little pause.)

EMILY: Even in New York in the eighties, *that* is strange.
    Keep breathing. Stop moving. STAY PUT. *(She exits)*

HANNAH *(Standing to go)*: I should go.

PRIOR: I'm not insane.

HANNAH: I didn't say you . . .

PRIOR: I saw an angel. That's insane.

HANNAH: Well, it's . . .

PRIOR: Insane. But I'm not insane. But then why did I do this to myself? Because I have been driven insane by . . . your son and by that lying. . . . Because ever since She arrived, ever since, I have been consumed by this ice-cold, razor-blade terror that just shouts and shouts "Keep moving! Run!" And I've run myself. . . . Into the ground. Right where She said I'd eventually be.

She seemed so real. What's happened to me?

(Little pause.)

HANNAH: You had a vision.

PRIOR: A vision. Thank you, Maria Ouspenskaya.

I'm not so far gone I can be assuaged by pity and lies.

HANNAH: I don't have pity. It's just not something I have.

(Little pause)

One hundred and seventy years ago, which is recent, an angel of God appeared to Joseph Smith in upstate New York, not far from here. People have visions.

PRIOR: But that's preposterous, that's . . .

HANNAH: It's not polite to call other people's beliefs preposterous.

He had great need of understanding. Our Prophet. His desire made prayer. His prayer made an angel. The angel was real. I believe that.

PRIOR: I don't. And I'm sorry but it's repellent to me. So much of what you believe.

HANNAH: What do I believe?

PRIOR: I'm a homosexual. With AIDS. I can just imagine what you . . .

HANNAH: No you can't. Imagine. The things in my head. You don't make assumptions about me, mister; I won't make them about you.

PRIOR *(A beat; he looks at her, then)*: Fair enough.

HANNAH: My son is . . . well, like you.

PRIOR: Homosexual.

235

HANNAH *(A nod, then)*: I flew into a rage when he told me, mad as hornets. At first I assumed it was about his . . . *(She shrugs)*

PRIOR: Homosexuality.

HANNAH: But that wasn't it. Homosexuality. It just seems . . . ungainly. Two men together. It isn't an appetizing notion but then, for me, men in *any* configuration . . . well they're so lumpish and stupid. And stupidity gets me cross.

PRIOR: I wish you would be more true to your demographic profile. Life is confusing enough.

(Little pause. They look at each other.)

PRIOR: You know the Bible, you know . . .

HANNAH: Reasonably well, I . . .

PRIOR: The prophets in the Bible, do they . . . ever refuse their vision?

HANNAH: There's scriptural precedent, yes.

PRIOR: And what does God do to them? When they do that?

HANNAH: He. . . . Well, he feeds them to whales.

(They both laugh. Prior's laugh brings on breathing trouble.)

HANNAH: Just lie still. You'll be all right.

PRIOR: No. I won't be. My lungs are getting tighter. The fever mounts and you get delirious. And then days of delirium and awful pain and drugs; you start slipping and then.
    I really . . . fucked up. I'm scared. I can't do it again.

HANNAH: You shouldn't talk that way. You ought to make a better show of yourself.

PRIOR: Look at this . . . horror.
    (He lifts his shirt; his torso is spotted with three or four lesions)

See? That's not human. That's why I run. Wouldn't you? Wouldn't anybody.

HANNAH: It's a cancer. Nothing more. Nothing more human than that.

PRIOR: Oh God, I want to be done.

HANNAH: An angel is just a belief, with wings and arms that can carry you. It's naught to be afraid of. If it lets you down, reject it. Seek for something new.

PRIOR: I . . .

(He stirs uncomfortably, adjusts his lap.)

PRIOR: Oh my.

HANNAH: What?

PRIOR: Listen.

(Distant thunder.)

PRIOR: It's Her. Oh my God.

HANNAH: It's the spring rain is all.

PRIOR: Stay with me.

HANNAH: Oh no, I . . .

PRIOR: You comfort me, you do, you stiffen my spine.

HANNAH: When I got up this morning this is not how I envisioned the day would end.

I'm not needed elsewhere.

PRIOR: If I sleep, will you keep watch?

She's approaching.

HANNAH: She is?

PRIOR *(Nodding his head "yes")*: Modesty forbids me explaining exactly *how* I know, but. . . . I have an infallible barometer of her proximity. And it's rising.

Scene 7

That night. Harper and Joe at home, in bed. A silence, then:

HARPER: When we have sex. Why do you keep your eyes closed?

JOE: I don't.

HARPER: You always do. You can say why, I already know the answer.

JOE: Then why do I have to . . .

HARPER: You imagine things. Imagine men.

JOE: Yes.

HARPER: Imagining, just like me, except the only time I wasn't imagining was when I was with you. You, the one part of the real world I wasn't allergic to.

JOE: Please. Don't.

HARPER: But I only *thought* I wasn't dreaming.

(Joe sits up abruptly, turns his back to her. Then he starts to put on his pants.)

HARPER: Oh. Oh. Back in Brooklyn, back with . . . *(The unsaid word is "Joe")*

JOE *(Not looking at her)*: I'm going out. I have to get some stuff I left behind.

HARPER: Look at me.

(He doesn't. He keeps dressing.)

HARPER: Look at me.
   Look at me.
   (Loud) HERE! LOOK HERE AT . . .

JOE *(Looking at her)*: What?

HARPER: What do you see?
JOE: What do I . . . ?
HARPER: What do you see?
JOE: *Nothing*, I . . .

(*Little pause.*)

HARPER: Thank you.
JOE: For what?
HARPER: Finally. The truth.
JOE (*A beat, then*): I'm going. Out. Just. . . . Out.

(*He exits.*)

HARPER: It sets you free.
    Goodbye.

Scene 8

Later that night. Louis in his apartment. He has a thick file full of Xeroxed articles. He is reading. Joe enters. They stare at each other.

LOUIS: Have you no decency, sir? At long last? Have you no sense of decency?
    Who said that?
JOE: Who said . . . ?
LOUIS: Who said, "Have you no . . ."
JOE: I don't. . . . I've come back. Please let me in.
LOUIS: You're in.

JOE: I'm having a very hard time, Louis.

It's so good to see you again.

LOUIS: You *really* don't know who said, "Have you no decency?"

JOE: What's wrong? Why are you . . .

LOUIS: OK, second question: *Have* you no decency?

Guess what I spent the rainy afternoon doing?

JOE: What?

LOUIS: My homework. Research at the courthouse. Look what I got: the Decisions of Justice Theodore Wilson, Second Circuit Court of Appeals. 1981–1984. The Reagan Years.

JOE: You, um, you read my decisions.

(Little pause.)

LOUIS: *Your* decisions. Yes.

The librarian was gay, he had all the good dish, he told me that Justice Wilson didn't write these opinions any more than Nixon wrote *Six Crises* . . .

JOE: Or Kennedy wrote *Profiles in Courage.*

LOUIS: Or Reagan wrote *Where's the Rest of Me?* Or you and I wrote the Book of Love.

JOE *(Trying to soothe things, going to Louis)*: Listen, I don't want to do this now. I mean it, I need you to stop attacking and . . .

(Louis shoves Joe away, hard.)

JOE: Hey!

LOUIS: These gems were ghostwritten. By you: his obedient, eager clerk. Naturally I was eager to read them.

JOE: Free country.

LOUIS: I love the one where you found against those women on Staten Island who were suing the New Jersey factory, the toothpaste makers whose orange-colored smoke was *blinding children* . . .

JOE: Not blind, just minor irritation.

LOUIS: Three of them had to be *hospitalized. Joe.* It's sort of brilliant, in a satanic sort of way, how you conclude that these women have no right to sue under the Air and Water Protection Act because the Air and Water Protection Act doesn't protect *people*, but actually only *air and water*! Amazing!

(Flipping through the cases) Have you no decency, have you no . . .

JOE: I don't believe this. My opinions are being criticized by the guy who changes the coffee filters in the secretaries' lounge!

LOUIS: But my *absolute favorite* is this:

Stephens versus the United States: the army guy who got a dishonorable discharge—for being gay. Now as I understand it, this Stephens had told the army he was gay when he enlisted, but when he got ready to retire they booted him out. Cheat the queer of his pension.

JOE: Right. And he sued. And he won the case. He got the pension back. So what are you . . .

LOUIS: The first judges gave him his pension back, *yes*, because: They ruled that gay men are members of a legitimate minority, entitled to the special protection of the Fourteenth Amendment of the U.S. Constitution. Equal Protection under the Law.

So then all the judges on the Second Circuit were assembled, and . . .

JOE: We found for the guy again.

LOUIS: But but but!

On an equitable estoppel. I had to look that up, I'm Mr. Coffee, I can't be expected to know these things.

They didn't change the *decision*, they just changed the *reason for* the decision. Right? They gave it to him on a technicality: The army knew Stephens was gay when he enlisted. That's all, that's why he won. Not because it's unconstitutional to discriminate against homosexuals. Because homosexuals, they write, are *not* entitled to equal protection under the law.

JOE: You're being really melodramatic, as usual, you . . .

LOUIS: Actually *they* didn't write this. You did. They gave this opinion to Wilson to write, which since they *know* he's a vegetable incapable of writing do-re-mi, was quite the vote of confidence in his industrious little clerk. This is an important bit of legal fag-bashing, isn't it? They trusted you to do it. And you didn't disappoint.

JOE: It's law not justice, it's power, not the merits of its exercise, it's not an expression of the ideal, it's . . .

LOUIS: So who said, "Have you no decency?"

JOE: I'm leaving.

LOUIS: You moron, how can you not know that?

JOE *(Overlapping)*: I'm leaving, you . . . son of a bitch, get out of my . . .

LOUIS: It's only the greatest punchline in American history.

JOE: Out of my way, Louis.

LOUIS: *"Have you no decency, at long last, sir, have you no decency at all?"*

JOE: I DON'T KNOW WHO SAID IT! WHY ARE YOU DOING THIS TO ME! *I LOVE YOU. I LOVE YOU.* WHY . . .

LOUIS: JOSEPH WELCH, THE ARMY/McCARTHY HEARINGS. Ask ROY. He'll tell you. He knows. He was *there*.

Roy Cohn. What I want to know is, did you fuck him?

JOE: Did I what?

LOUIS: How often has the latex-sheathed cock I put in my mouth been previously in the mouth of the most evil, twisted, vicious bastard ever to snort coke at Studio 54, because lips that kissed those lips will never kiss mine.

JOE: Don't worry about that, just get out of the . . .

(Joe tries to push Louis aside; Louis pushes back, forcefully.)

LOUIS: Did you fuck him, did he pay you to let him . . .

JOE: MOVE!

(Louis throws the Xeroxes in Joe's face. They fly everywhere. Joe pushes Louis, Louis grabs Joe.)

LOUIS: You *lied* to me, you *love* me, well fuck you, you cheap piece of . . .

(Joe slugs Louis in the stomach, hard. Louis goes to his knees, then starts to stand up again, badly winded.)

LOUIS: He's got AIDS! Did you even *know* that? Stupid closeted bigots, you probably never figured out that each other was . . .

JOE: Shut up.

(Joe punches Louis again.)

LOUIS: Fascist hypocrite lying filthy . . .

(Louis tries to hit Joe, and Joe starts to hit Louis repeatedly. Louis clings to Joe as he punches away.)

LOUIS *(Going to the floor)*: Oh jeeesus, aw jeez, oh . . .

(Louis falls to the floor. Joe stands over him.)

JOE: Now stop. . . . Now stop. . . . I . . .
 Please. Say you're OK, please. *Please.*
LOUIS *(Not moving)*: That. . . . Hurt.
JOE: I never did that before, I never hit anyone before, I . . .

(Louis sits up. His mouth and eye have been cut.)

JOE: Can you open it? Can you see?
LOUIS: I can see blood.
JOE: Let me get a towel, let me . . .
LOUIS *(Pushing Joe away)*: I could have you arrested you. . . .
 Creep.
 They'd think I put you in jail for beating me up.
JOE: I never hit anyone before, I . . .
LOUIS: But it'd really be for those decisions.
 It was like a sex scene in an Ayn Rand novel, huh?
JOE: *I hurt you!* I'm sorry, Louis, I never hit anyone before, I . . .
LOUIS: Yeah yeah get lost. Before I really lose my temper and
 hurt you back.
 I just want to lie here and bleed for a while. Do me
 good.

Scene 9

*Later that night. Roy in a very serious hospital bed, monitor-
ing machines and IV drips galore. Ethel appears.*

ROY *(Singing softly)*:
 John Brown's Body lies a-moulderin' in the grave,
 John Brown's Body lies a-moulderin' in the grave,

John Brown's Body lies a-moulderin' in the grave,
His truth is marching on . . .

ETHEL: Look at that big smile. What you got to smile about, Roy?

ROY: I'm going, Ethel. Finally, finally done with this world, at long long last. All mine enemies will be standing on the other shore, mouths gaping open like stupid fish, while the Almighty parts the Sea of Death and lets his Royboy cross over to Jordan. On dry land and still a lawyer.

ETHEL: Don't count your chickens, Roy.

It's over.

ROY: Over?

ETHEL: I wanted the news should come from me.

The panel ruled against you Roy.

ROY: No, no, they only started meeting two days ago.

ETHEL: They recommended disbarment.

ROY: The Executive still has to rule . . . on the recommendation, it'll take another week to sort it out and before then . . .

ETHEL: The Executive was waiting, and they ruled, one two three. They accepted the panel's recommendation.

ROY: I'm . . .

ETHEL: One of the main guys on the Executive leaned over to his friend and said, "Finally. I've hated that little faggot for thirty-six years."

ROY: I'm. . . . They . . .

ETHEL: They won, Roy. You're not a lawyer anymore.

ROY: But am I dead?

ETHEL: No. They beat you. You lost.

(Pause)

I decided to come here so I could see could I forgive you. You who I have hated so terribly I have borne my hatred for you up into the heavens and made a needle-sharp little star in the sky out of it. It's the star of Ethel

Rosenberg's Hatred, and it burns every year for one night only, June Nineteen. It burns acid green.

I came to forgive but all I can do is take pleasure in your misery. Hoping I'd get to see you die more terrible than I did. And you are, 'cause you're dying in shit, Roy, defeated. And you could kill me, but you couldn't ever defeat me. You never won. And when you die all anyone will say is: Better he had never lived at all.

(Pause.)

ROY: Ma?

Muddy? Is it . . . ?

(He sits up, looks at Ethel) Ma?

ETHEL *(Uncertain, then)*: It's Ethel, Roy.

ROY: Muddy? I feel bad.

ETHEL *(Looking around)*: Who are you talking to, Roy, it's . . .

ROY: Good to see you, Ma, it's been years.

I feel bad. Sing to me.

ETHEL: I'm not your mother Roy.

ROY: It's cold in here, I'm up so late, past my time.

Don't be mad Ma but I'm scared . . . ? A little.

Don't be mad. Sing me a song. Please.

ETHEL: I don't want to Roy, I'm not your . . .

ROY: Please, it's scary out here. *(He starts to cry)*

(He sinks back) Oh God. Oh God, I'm so sorry . . .

ETHEL *(Singing, very soft)*:

Shteit a bocher

Un er tracht,

Tracht un tracht

A gantze nacht:

Vemen tzu nemen

Um nit farshemen

Vemen tsu nemen,
Um nit farshem.
Tum-ba-la, Tum-ba-la, Tum-balalaike,
Tum-ba-la, Tum-ba-la, Tum-balalaike,
Tum Balalaike, shpil balalaike . . .
(Pause)
Roy . . . ? Are you . . . ?
(She crosses to the bed, looks at him. Goes back to her chair)
That's it.

(Belize enters, goes to the bed.)

BELIZE: Wake up, it's time to . . .

Oh. Oh, you're . . .

ROY *(Sitting up violently)*: No I'm NOT!

I fooled you Ethel, I knew who you were all along, I can't believe you fell for that ma stuff, I just wanted to see if I could finally, finally make Ethel Rosenberg sing! I WIN!

(He falls back on the bed)

Oh fuck, oh fuck me I . . .

(In a very faint voice) Next time around: I don't want to be a man. I wanna be an octopus. Remember that, OK? A fucking . . . *(Punching an imaginary button with his finger)* Hold.

(He dies.)

ACT FIVE:

Heaven, I'm in Heaven

February 1986

Scene 1

Very late, same night. Prior's hospital room. Hannah is sleeping in a chair. Prior is standing on his bed. There's an eerie light on him. Hannah stirs, moans a little, wakes up suddenly, sees him.

PRIOR: She's on her way.

(The lights drain to black.)

HANNAH: Turn the lights back on, turn the lights . . .

(There is the sound of a silvery trumpet in the dark, and a tattoo of faraway drums. Silence. Thunder. Then all over the walls, Hebrew letters appear, writhing in flames. The scene is lit by their light. The Angel is there, suddenly. She is dressed in black and looks terrifying. Hannah screams and buries her face in her hands.)

ANGEL:

> I I I I Have Returned, Prophet,
> *(Thunder)*
> And not according to Plan.

PRIOR: Take it back.

> *(Big thunderclap)*
> The Book, whatever you left in me, I won't be its repository, I reject it.
> *(Thunder. To Hannah:)*
> Help me out here. HELP ME!

HANNAH *(Trying to shut it all out)*: I don't, I don't, this is a dream it's a dream it's a . . .

PRIOR: I don't think that's really the point right at this particular moment.

HANNAH: I don't know what to . . .

PRIOR *(Overlap)*: Well it was your idea, reject the vision you said and . . .

HANNAH *(Overlap)*: Yes but I thought it was more a . . . metaphorical. . . . I . . .

PRIOR *(Overlap)*: You said scriptural precedent, you said. . . . WHAT AM I SUPPOSED TO . . .

HANNAH *(Overlap)*: You . . . you . . . wrestle her.

PRIOR: SAY *WHAT*?

HANNAH: It's an angel, you . . . just . . . grab hold and say . . . oh what was it, wait, wait, umm. . . . OH! Grab her, say "I will not let thee go except thou bless me!" Then wrestle with her till she gives in.

PRIOR: YOU wrestle her, I don't know how to wrestle, I . . .

(The Angel flies up into the air and lands right in front of Prior. Prior grabs her—she emits a terrible, impossibly loud, shuddering eagle-screech. Prior and the Angel wrestle.)

PRIOR: I . . . will not let thee go except thou bless me. Take back your Book. Anti-Migration, that's so feeble, I can't believe you couldn't do better than that, free me, unfetter me, bless me or whatever but I will be let go.

ANGEL *(This should be a whole chorus of voices)*:

I I I I Am the

CONTINENTAL PRINCIPALITY OF AMERICA, I I I I

AM THE BIRD OF PREY I Will NOT BE COM- PELLED, I . . .

(There is a great blast of music and a shaft of white light streams in through the blue murk. Within this incredibly bright column of light there is a ladder of even brighter, purer light, reaching up into infinity. At the conjunctions of each rung there are flaming alephs.)

ANGEL:

Entrance has been gained. Return the Text to Heaven.

PRIOR *(Terrified)*: Can I come back? I don't want to go unless . . .

ANGEL *(Angry)*:

You have prevailed, Prophet. You. . . . Choose.

Now release me.

I have torn a muscle in my thigh.

PRIOR: Big deal, my leg's been hurting for months.

(He releases the Angel. He hesitates. He ascends.

The room is instantly plunged into near darkness. The Angel turns her attention to Hannah.)

HANNAH: What? What? You've got no business with me, I didn't call you, you're *his* fever dream not mine, and he's

gone now and you should go too, I'm waking up right. . . .
NOW!

(Nothing happens. The Angel spreads her wings. The room becomes red hot. The Angel extends her hands towards Hannah. Hannah walks towards her, torn between immense unfamiliar desire and fear. Hannah kneels. The Angel kisses her on the forehead and then the lips—a long, hot kiss.)

ANGEL: The Body is the Garden of the Soul.

(Hannah has an enormous orgasm, as the Angel flies away to the accompanying glissando of a baroque piccolo trumpet.)

Scene 2

Prior Walter is in Heaven. He is dressed in prophet robes reminiscent of Charlton Heston's Moses drag in The Ten Commandments. *Prior is carrying the Book of the Anti-Migratory Epistle. Heaven looks mostly like San Francisco after the Great 1906 Quake. It has a deserted, derelict feel to it, rubble is strewn everywhere. Seated on a wooden crate on a street corner is Harper, playing with a cat.*

HARPER: Oh! It's you! My imaginary friend.
PRIOR: What are you doing here? Are you dead?
HARPER: No, I just had sex, I'm not dead! Why? Where are we?
PRIOR: Heaven.
HARPER: Heaven? I'm in Heaven?
PRIOR: That cat! That's Little Sheba!

HARPER: She was wandering around. Everyone here wanders. Or they sit on crates, playing card games. Heaven. Holy moly.

PRIOR: How did Sheba die?

HARPER: Rat poison, hit by a truck, fight with an alley cat, cancer, another truck, old age, fell in the East River, heartworms and one last truck.

PRIOR: Then it's true? Cats really have nine lives?

HARPER: That was a joke. I don't know how she died, I don't talk to cats I'm not that crazy. Just upset. We had sex, and then he . . . had to go. I drank an enormous glass of water and two Valiums. Or six. Maybe I overdosed, like Marilyn Monroe.

Did you die?

PRIOR: No, I'm here on business.

I can return to the world. If I want to.

HARPER: Do you?

PRIOR: I don't know.

HARPER: I know. Heaven is depressing, full of dead people and all, but life.

PRIOR: To face loss. With grace. Is key, I think, but it's impossible. All you ever do is lose and lose.

HARPER: But not letting go deforms you so.

PRIOR: The world's too hard. Stay here. With me.

HARPER: I can't. I feel like shit but I've never felt more alive. I've finally found the secret of all that Mormon energy. Devastation. That's what makes people migrate, build things. Heartbroken people do it, people who have lost love. Because I don't think God loves His people any better than Joe loved me. The string was cut, and off they went.

I have to go home now. I hope you come back. *Look* at this place. Can you imagine spending eternity here?

PRIOR: It's supposed to look like San Francisco.

HARPER *(Looking around)*: Ugh.

PRIOR: Oh but the real San Francisco, on earth, is unspeakably beautiful.

HARPER: Unspeakable beauty.

That's something I would like to see.

(Harper and Sheba vanish.)

PRIOR: Oh! She. . . . She took the cat. Come back, you took the . . .

(Little pause)

Goodbye little Sheba. Goodbye.

(The scenery dissolves and is replaced by an interior. A great antechamber to the Hall of the Upper Orders. It looks remarkably like the San Francisco City Hall, with much cracked plaster. The Angel is standing there.)

ANGEL: Greetings, Prophet. We have been waiting for you.

Scene 3

Two AM. Roy's hospital room. Roy's body is on the bed. Ethel is sitting in a chair. Belize enters, then calls off in a whisper:

BELIZE: Hurry.

(Louis enters wearing an overcoat and dark sunglasses.)

LOUIS: Oh my god, oh my god it's—oh this is too weird for words, it's Roy Cohn, it's . . . so *creepy* here, I hate hospitals, I . . .

BELIZE: *Stop whining.* We have to move fast, I'm supposed to call the duty nurse if his condition changes and . . . *(He looks at Roy)* It's changed.

Take off those glasses you look ridiculous.

(Louis takes off the glasses. He has two black eyes, one cut.)

BELIZE: What happened to *you?*

(Belize touches the swelling near Louis's eye.)

LOUIS: OW OW! *(He waves Belize's hand away)* Expiation. For my sins.

What am I doing here?

BELIZE: Expiation for your sins. I can't take the stuff out myself, I have to tell them he's dead and fill out all the forms, and I don't want them confiscating the medicine. I needed a packmule, so I called you.

LOUIS: Why me? You hate me.

BELIZE: I needed a Jew. You were the first to come to mind.

LOUIS: What do you mean you needed . . .

BELIZE: We're going to thank him. For the pills.

LOUIS: *Thank him?*

BELIZE: What do you call the Jewish prayer for the dead?

LOUIS: The Kaddish?

BELIZE: That's the one. Hit it.

LOUIS: Whoah, hold on.

BELIZE: Do it, do it, they'll be in here to check and he . . .

LOUIS: I'm not saying any fucking Kaddish for him. The drugs OK, sure, fine, but no fucking way am I praying for *him.* My New Deal Pinko Parents in Schenectady would never forgive me, they're already so disappointed, "He's a fag, he's an office temp, and *now look*, he's saying Kaddish for Roy Cohn." I can't believe you'd actually pray for . . .

BELIZE: Louis, I'd even pray for you.

He was a terrible person. He died a hard death. So maybe. . . . A queen can forgive her vanquished foe. It isn't easy, it doesn't count if it's easy, it's the hardest thing. Forgiveness. Which is maybe where love and justice finally meet. Peace, at least. Isn't that what the Kaddish asks for?

LOUIS: Oh it's Hebrew who knows what it's asking?[1]

(Little pause. Louis and Belize look at each other and then Louis looks at Roy, staring at him unflinchingly for the first time.)

LOUIS *(Looking at Roy)*: I'm thirty-two years old and I've never been in a room with a dead body before. *(Louis touches Roy's forehead)* It's so heavy, and small. I know probably less of the Kaddish than you do, Belize, I'm an intensely secular Jew, I didn't even Bar Mitzvah.

BELIZE: Do the best you can.

(Louis puts a Kleenex on his head.)

LOUIS: Yisgadal ve'yiskadash sh'mey rabo, sh'mey de kidshoh, uh. . . . Boray pre hagoffen. No, that's the Kiddush, not the. . . . Um, shema Yisroel adonai. . . . This is silly, Belize, I can't . . .

ETHEL *(Standing, softly)*: B'olmo deevro chiroosey ve'yamlich malchusey . . .

---

[1] Author's note: I know, I know, it's not Hebrew, it's Aramaic, but for the sake of the joke . . .

LOUIS: B'olmo deevro chiroosey ve'yamlich malchusey . . .

ETHEL: Bechayeychon uv'yomechechon uvchayey d'chol beys Yisroel . . .

LOUIS: Bechayeychon uv'yomechechon uvchayey d'chol beys Yisroel . . .

ETHEL: Ba'agolo uvizman koriv . . .

LOUIS: Ve'imroo omain.

ETHEL: Yehey sh'mey rabo m'vorach . . .

LOUIS AND ETHEL: L'olam ulolmey olmayoh. Yisborach ve'yishtabach ve'yispoar ve'yisroman ve'yisnasey ve'yis'hadar ve'yisalleh ve'yishallol sh'mey dekudsho . . .

ETHEL: Berich hoo le'eylo min kol birchoso veshiroso . . .

LOUIS AND ETHEL: Tushb'choso venechemoso, daameeron b'olmo ve'imroo omain. Y'he sh'lomo rabbo min sh'mayo v'chayim olenu v'al kol Yisroel, v'imru omain . . .

ETHEL: Oseh sholom bimromov, hu ya-aseh sholom olenu v'al col Yisroel . . .

LOUIS: Oseh sholom bimromov, hu ya-aseh sholom olenu v'al col Yisroel . . .

ETHEL: V'imru omain.

LOUIS: V'imru omain.

ETHEL: You sonofabitch.

LOUIS: You sonofabitch.

(Ethel vanishes.)

BELIZE: Thank you Louis, you did fine.

LOUIS: Fine? What are you talking about, fine? That was fucking miraculous.

Scene 4

Two AM. Joe enters the empty Brooklyn apartment, carrying the suitcase from Louis's.

JOE: I'm back. Harper?
      (He switches on a light)
      Harper?

(Roy enters from the bedroom, dressed in a fabulous floor-length black velvet robe de chambre. Joe starts with terror, turns away, then looks again. Roy's still there. Joe is completely frightened.)

JOE: What are you doing here?
ROY: Dead Joe doesn't matter.
JOE: No, no, you're not here, you . . .
      You lied to me. You said cancer, you said . . .
ROY: You could have read it in the papers. AIDS. I didn't want you to get the wrong impression.
      You feel bad that you beat somebody.
JOE: I want you to . . .
ROY: He deserved it.
JOE: No he didn't he . . .
ROY: Everybody does. Everybody could use a good beating.
JOE: I *hurt* him. I didn't . . . mean to, I didn't want to but . . . I made him bleed. And he won't . . . ever see me again, I won't . . .
      Louis.
      (Joe starts to cry)
      Oh God, please go, Roy, you're really frightening me, please please go.
      Harper.

ROY: Show me a little of what you've learned, baby Joe. Out in the world.

(Roy kisses Joe softly on the mouth.)

ROY: Damn.

I gotta shuffle off this mortal coil. I hope they have something for me to do in the Great Hereafter, I get bored easy.

You'll find, my friend, that what you love will take you places you never dreamed you'd go.

(Roy vanishes. Harper enters. Joe and Harper stare at each other.)

HARPER: Hope you didn't worry.
JOE: Harper?

Where . . . .Were you . . .
HARPER: A trip to the moon on gossamer wings.
JOE: What?
HARPER: You ought to get your hearing checked, you say that a lot.

I was out. With a friend. In Paradise.

Scene 5

Heaven: in the Council Room of the Continental Principalities. As the scene is being set, a Voice (the same as in Act One Scene 1 and Act Three Scene 3) proclaims:

VOICE: In the Hall of the Continental Principalities; Heaven, a City Much Like San Francisco. Six of Seven Myriad

Infinite Aggregate Angelic Entities in Attendance, May Their Glorious Names Be Praised Forever and Ever, Hallelujah. Permanent Emergency Council is now in Session.

(The Continental Principalities sit around a table covered with a heavy tapestry on which is woven an ancient map of the world. The tabletop is covered with archaic and broken astronomical, astrological, mathematical and nautical objects of measurement and calculation; heaps and heaps and heaps of books and files and bundles of yellowing newspapers; inkpots, clay tablets, styli and quill pens. The great chamber is dimly lit by candles and a single great bulb overhead, the light of which pulses to the audible rhythmic surgings and waverings of a great unseen generator.

At the center of the table is a single bulky radio, a 1940s model in very poor repair. It is switched on and glowing, and the Angels are gathered about it, intent upon its dim, crackly signal.)

RADIO *(In a British accent)*: . . . one week following the explosion at the number four reactor, the fires are still burning and an estimated . . . *(Static)* . . . releasing into the atmosphere fifty million curies of radioactive iodine, six million curies of caesium and strontium rising in a plume over five miles high, carried by the winds over an area stretching from the Urals to thousands of miles beyond Soviet borders, it . . . *(Static)* . . .

ANTARCTICA: When?

OCEANIA: April 26th. Sixty-two days from today.

ASIATICA: Where is this place? This *(With great loathing)* reactor?

EUROPA: Chernobyl. In Belarus.

(The static intensifies.)

ASIATICA: We are losing the signal.

(The Angels make mystic gestures. The signal returns.)

RADIO: . . . falling like toxic snow into the Dnieper River, which provides drinking water for thirty-five million Russians. Radioactive debris contaminating over three hundred thousand hectares of topsoil for a minimum of thirty years, and . . . *(Static)* . . . now hearing of thousands of workers who have absorbed fifty times the lethal dose of . . . *(Static)* . . . BBC Radio, reporting live from Chernobyl, on the eighth day of the . . .

(The radio signal is engulfed in white noise and fades out. There is a long silence.)

OCEANIA: It is unholy.
AFRICANII: This Age is the threnody chant of a Poet,
    A dark-devising Poet whose only theme is Death.
EUROPA: Hundreds, thousands will die.
OCEANIA: Horribly. Hundreds of thousands.
AFRICANII: Millions.
ANTARCTICA: Let them. Uncountable multitudes. Horrible. It is by their own hands. I I I will rejoice to see it.
AUSTRALIA *(A polite but firm reprimand)*: That is forbidden us. Silence in Heaven.

(Some of the Angels cough, some make mystic signs.)

ASIATICA: This radio is a terrible radio.

AUSTRALIA: The reception is too weak.

AFRICANII: A vacuum tube has died.

ASIATICA: Can it be fixed?

AUSTRALIA: It is Beyond Us.

ASIATICA: However, I I I I I I I would like to know. What is a vacuum tube?

OCEANIA: It is a simple diode.

ASIATICA: Aha.

AFRICANII: Within are an anode and a cathode. The positive electrons travel from the cathode across voltage fields . . .

OCEANIA: The cathode is, in fact, negatively charged.

AFRICANII: No, positive, I I I I . . . *(She looks inside the radio)*

EUROPA: This device ought never to have been brought here. It is a Pandemonium.

ANTARCTICA: I I I agree. In diodes we see manifest the self-same divided Human consciousness which has engendered the multifarious catastrophes to which We are impotent witness . . .

AFRICANII: You are correct, it is negative. Regardless of the charge, it is the absence of resistance in a vacuum which . . .

ANTARCTICA *(Overlapping)*: I I I do not weep for *them*, I I I I weep for the vexation of the Blank Spaces, I weep for the Dancing Light, for the irremediable wastage of Fossil Fuels, Old Blood of the Globe spilled wantonly or burned and jettisoned onto the Crystal Air . . .

EUROPA *(Overlapping on "wastage")*: Between this crippled gadget and the mephitic plumes of that Diabolus, that *reactor*, there is not a scintilla of difference.

OCEANIA: Yes but without it, Oh Most Glorious Intelligences, how would we maintain surveillance over Human Mischief? With *this*?

(He brandishes an astrolabe)

AUSTRALIA: It is a Conundrum, We cannot solve Conundrums, if only He would return, I I I I do not know whether We have erred in transporting these dubious Inventions, but. . . . If We refer to His Codex of Procedure, I I I I cannot recall which page but . . .

(There is an enormous peal of thunder and a blaze of lightning. Prior and the Angel of America are in the chamber, standing before the council table.
The Principalities stare at Prior.)

ANGEL: Most August Fellow Principalities, Angels Most High: I regret my absence at this session, I was detained.

(Pause.)

AUSTRALIA: Ah, this is . . . ?
ANGEL: The Prophet. Yes.
AUSTRALIA: Ah.

(The Angels bow.)

EUROPA: We were working.
AFRICANII: Making Progress.

(Thunderclap.)

PRIOR: I. . . . I want to return this.

(He holds out the Book. No one takes it from him.)

AUSTRALIA: What is the matter with it?
PRIOR *(A beat, then)*: It just. . . . It just. . . . We can't just stop. We're not rocks—progress, migration, motion is . . .

modernity. It's *animate*, it's what living things do. We desire. Even if all we desire is stillness, it's still desire *for*. Even if we go faster than we should. We can't *wait*. And wait for what? God . . .

(Thunderclap.)

PRIOR: God . . .

(Thunderclap.)

PRIOR: He isn't coming back.
　　And even if He did . . . .
　　If He ever did come back, if He ever *dared* to show His face, or his Glyph or whatever in the Garden again . . . if after all this destruction, if after all the terrible days of this terrible century He returned to see ⋮ . . . how much suffering His abandonment had created, if all He has to offer is death, you should *sue* the bastard. That's my only contribution to all this Theology. Sue the bastard for walking out. How dare He.

(Pause.)

ANGEL: Thus spake the Prophet.
PRIOR *(Starting to put the Book on the table)*: So thank you . . .
　　for sharing this with me, but I don't want to keep it.
OCEANIA *(To the Angel of America)*: He wants to live.
PRIOR: Yes.
　　I'm thirty years old, for God sake. *(Softer rumble)* I haven't *done* anything yet, I . . .
　　I want to be healthy again. And this plague, it should stop. In me and everywhere. Make it go away.

AUSTRALIA:

Oh We have tried.
We suffer with You but
We do not know. We
Do not know how.

(Prior and Australia look at each other.)

EUROPA:

This is the Tome of Immobility, of respite, of cessation.
Drink of its bitter water once, Prophet, and never
thirst again.

PRIOR: I . . . can't.

*(Prior puts the Book on the table. He removes his prophet
robes, revealing the hospital gown underneath. He places the
robe by the Book)*

I still want. . . . My blessing. Even sick. I want to be
alive.

ANGEL:

You only think you do.
Life is a habit with you.
You have not *seen* what is to come:
We *have*:
What will the grim Unfolding of these Latter Days
bring?
That you or any Being should wish to endure them?
Death more plenteous than all Heaven has tears to
mourn it,
The slow dissolving of the Great Design,
The spiraling apart of the Work of Eternity,
The World and its beautiful particle logic
All collapsed. All dead, forever,
In starless, moonlorn onyx night.

We are failing, failing,
The Earth and the Angels.

(The sound of a great generator, failing. The lights dim.)

ANGEL:

Look up, look up,
It is Not-to-Be Time.
Oh who asks of the Orders Blessing
With Apocalypse Descending?
Who demands: More Life?
When Death like a Protector
Blinds our eyes, shielding from tender nerve
More horror than can be borne.
Let any Being on whom Fortune smiles
Creep away to Death
Before that last dreadful daybreak
When all your ravaging returns to you
With the rising, scorching, unrelenting Sun:
When morning blisters crimson
And bears all life away,
A tidal wave of Protean Fire
That curls around the planet
And bares the Earth clean as bone.

(Pause.)

PRIOR: But still. Still.
Bless me anyway.
I want more life. I can't help myself. I do.
I've lived through such terrible times, and there are
people who live through much much worse, but. . . . You
see them living anyway. When they're more spirit than

body, more sores than skin, when they're burned and in agony, when flies lay eggs in the corners of the eyes of their children, they live. Death usually has to *take* life away. I don't know if that's just the animal. I don't know if it's not braver to die. But I recognize the habit. The addiction to being alive. We live past hope. If I can find hope anywhere, that's it, that's the best I can do. It's so much not enough, so inadequate but. . . . Bless me anyway. I want more life.

(He begins to exit.
The Angels, unseen by Prior, make a mystical sign. He turns again to face them.)

PRIOR: And if He returns, take Him to Court. He walked out on us. He ought to pay.

Scene 6

On the streets of Heaven. Rabbi Isidor Chemelwitz and Sarah Ironson are seated on wooden crates with another crate between them. They are playing cards. Prior enters.
(This scene is optional.)

PRIOR: Excuse me, I'm looking for a way out of this, do you . . . Oh! You're . . .
SARAH IRONSON *(To the Rabbi)*: Vos vil er? [What does he want?]
RABBI ISIDOR CHEMELWITZ: Di goyim, zey veysn nisht vi zikh oyftsufirn. [These Gentiles, they have no manners.]

PRIOR: Are you Sarah Ironson?

(She looks up at him.)

PRIOR: I was at your funeral! You look just like your grandson, Louis. I know him. Louis. He never wanted you to find out, but did you know he's gay?

SARAH IRONSON *(Not understanding)*: Vi? [What?]

RABBI ISIDOR CHEMELWITZ: Dein aynickl, Louis? [Your grandson, Louis?]

SARAH IRONSON: Yeah?

RABBI ISIDOR CHEMELWITZ *(Sotto voce)*: Er iz a feygele.

SARAH IRONSON: A *feygele*? Oy.

RABBI ISIDOR CHEMELWITZ *(To Sarah)*: Itst gistu. [You deal.]

PRIOR: Why does everyone here play cards?

RABBI ISIDOR CHEMELWITZ: Why? *(To Sarah)* Dos goy vil visn far-Vos mir shpiln in kortn. [The goy wants to know why we play cards.]

OK.

Cards is strategy but mostly a game of chance. In Heaven, everything is known. To the Great Questions are lying about here like yesterday's newspaper all the answers. So from what comes the pleasures of Paradise? *Indeterminacy!* Because mister, with the Angels, may their names be always worshipped and adored, it's all gloom and doom and give up already. But still is there Accident, in this pack of playing cards, still is there the Unknown, the Future. You understand me? It ain't all so much mechanical as they think.

You got another question?

PRIOR: I want to go home.

RABBI ISIDOR CHEMELWITZ: Oh simple. Here. To do this, every Kabbalist on earth would sell his right nut.

Penuel, Peniel, Ja'akov Beth-Yisroel, Killeeyou, killeemee, OOO-oooooooo-OOOO-oooooohmayn!

(The ladder, the music and the lights. Prior starts to descend.)

SARAH IRONSON: Hey! Zogt Loubeleh az di Bobbe zogt:

RABBI ISIDOR CHEMELWITZ: She says tell this Louis Grandma says:

SARAH IRONSON: Er iz tomid geven a bissele farblonjet, shoin vi a boytshikl. Ober siz nisht keyn antshuldigunk.

RABBI ISIDOR CHEMELWITZ: From when he was a boy he was always mixed up. But it's no excuse.

SARAH IRONSON: *He should have visited!* But I forgive. Tell him: az er darf ringen mit zain Libm Nomen. Yah?!

RABBI ISIDOR CHEMELWITZ: You should struggle with the Almighty.

SARAH IRONSON: Azoi toot a Yid.

RABBI ISIDOR CHEMELWITZ: It's the Jewish way.

Scene 7

It's morning, the next day. Prior descends from Heaven and slips into bed. Belize is sleeping in a chair.

PRIOR *(Waking)*: Oh.
    I'm exhausted.

BELIZE *(Waking)*: You've been working hard.

PRIOR: I feel terrible.

BELIZE: Welcome back to the world.

PRIOR: From where, I. . . . Oh. Oh I . . .

(Emily enters.)

EMILY: Well look at this. It's the dawn of man.

BELIZE: Venus rising from the sea.

PRIOR: I'm wet.

EMILY: Fever broke. That's a good sign, they'll be in to change you in . . .

PRIOR *(Looking around)*: Mrs. Pitt? Did she . . .

BELIZE: Elle fait sa toilette. Elle est *tres* formidable, ça. Where did you find her?

PRIOR: We found each other, she . . .

    I've had a remarkable dream. And you were there, and you . . .

(Hannah enters.)

PRIOR: And you.

HANNAH: I what?

PRIOR: And some of it was terrible, and some of it was wonderful, but all the same I kept saying I want to go home. And they sent me home.

HANNAH *(To Prior)*: What are you talking about?

PRIOR *(To Hannah)*: Thank you.

HANNAH: I just slept in the chair.

PRIOR *(To Belize)*: She saved my life.

HANNAH: I did no such thing, I slept in the chair. Being in hospital upsets me, it reminds me of things.

    I have to go home now. I had the most *peculiar* dream.

(There's a knock on the door. It opens. Louis enters.)

LOUIS: Can I come in?

(Brief tense pause; Prior looks at Louis and then at Belize.)

EMILY: I have to start rounds.

> *(To Prior)* You're one of the lucky ones. I could give you a rose. You rest your weary bones.

PRIOR *(To Lou)*: What are you . . .

> *(He sees Louis's cuts and bruises)* What happened to *you*?

LOUIS: Visible scars. You said . . .

PRIOR: Oh Louis, you're so goddamned literal about everything.

HANNAH: I'm going now.

PRIOR: You'll come back.

HANNAH *(A beat, then)*: If I can. I have things to take care of.

PRIOR: Please do.

> I have always depended on the kindness of strangers.

HANNAH: Well that's a stupid thing to do. *(Exits)*

LOUIS: Who's she?

PRIOR *(A beat, then)*: You really don't want to know.

BELIZE: Before I depart. A homecoming gift.

(Belize puts his shoulder bag in Prior's lap. Prior opens it; it's full of bottles of pills.)

PRIOR *(Squinting hard)*: What? I can't read the label, I . . .

> My eyes. Aren't any better.
>
> *(Squints even harder)* AZT?
>
> Where on earth did you. . . . These are hot pills. I am shocked.

BELIZE: A contribution to the get-well fund. From a bad fairy.

LOUIS: These pills, they . . . they make you better.

PRIOR: They're poison, they make you anemic.

> This is my life, from now on, Louis. I'm not getting "better."

(To Belize) I'm not sure I'm ready to do that to my bone marrow.

BELIZE *(Taking the bag)*: We can talk about it tomorrow. I'm going home to nurse my grudges. Ta, baby, sleep all day. Ta, Louis, you sure know how to clear a room. *(Belize exits)*

LOUIS: Prior.

I want to come back to you.

Scene 8

Same morning. Split scene: Lou and Prior in Prior's hospital room, as before; Harper and Joe in Brooklyn, as at the end of Act Five Scene 4.

HARPER: I want your credit card.

That's all. You can keep track of me from where the charges come from. If you want to keep track. I don't care.

JOE: I have some things to tell you.

HARPER: Oh we shouldn't talk. I don't want to do that anymore. Credit card.

JOE: I don't know what will happen to me without you. Only you. Only you love me. Out of everyone in the world. I have done things, I'm ashamed. But I have changed. I don't know how yet, but.... Please, please, don't leave me now.

Harper.

You're my good heart.

(She looks at him, she walks up to him and slaps him, hard.)

HARPER *(Quietly)*: Did that hurt?

(Joe nods "yes.")

HARPER: Yes. Remember that. Please.
     If I can get a job, or something, I'll cut the card to pieces. And there won't be charges anymore. Credit card.

(Joe takes out his wallet, gives her his card.)

JOE *(Small voice, not looking at her)*: Call or. . . . Call. You have to.

HARPER: No. Probably never again. That's how bad.
     Sometimes, maybe lost is best. Get lost. Joe. Go exploring.

(Harper digs in the sofa. She removes her Valium stash. She shakes out two pills, goes to Joe, takes his hand and puts the Valium in his open palm.)

HARPER: With a big glass of water. *(She leaves)*

LOUIS: I want to come back to you.
     You could . . . respond, you could say something, throw me out or say it's fine, or it's not fine but sure what the hell or . . .
     (Little pause)
     I really failed you. But . . . this is hard. Failing in love isn't the same as not loving. It doesn't let you off the hook, it doesn't mean . . . you're free to not love.

PRIOR: I love you Louis.

LOUIS: Good. I love you.

PRIOR: I really do.
     But you can't come back. Not ever.
     I'm sorry. But you can't.

Scene 9

Roy, in Heaven, or Hell or Purgatory—standing waist-deep in a smoldering pit, facing a great flaming Aleph, which bathes him and the whole theatre in a volcanic, pulsating red light. Underneath, a basso-profundo roar, like a thousand Bessemer furnaces going at once, deep underground.
(This scene is also optional.)

ROY: Paternity suit? Abandonment? Family court is my particular metier, I'm an absolute fucking demon with Family Law. Just tell me who the judge is, and what kind of jewelry does he like? If it's a jury, it's harder, juries take more talk but sometimes it's worth it, going jury, for what it saves you in bribes. Yes I will represent you, King of the Universe, yes I will sing and eviscerate, I will bully and seduce, I will win for you and make the plaintiffs, those traitors, wish they had never heard the name of . . .
(Huge thunderclap)
Is it a done deal, are we on? Good, then I gotta start by telling you you ain't got a case here, you're guilty as hell, no question, you have nothing to plead but not to worry, darling, I will make something up.

Scene 10

That night. Louis and Prior remain from the previous scene. Joe is sitting alone in Brooklyn. Harper appears. She is in a window seat on board a jumbo jet, airborne.

HARPER: Night flight to San Francisco. Chase the moon across America. God! It's been years since I was on a plane!

When we hit thirty-five thousand feet, we'll have reached the tropopause. The great belt of calm air. As close as I'll ever get to the ozone.

I dreamed we were there. The plane leapt the tropopause, the safe air, and attained the outer rim, the ozone, which was ragged and torn, patches of it threadbare as old cheesecloth, and that was frightening . . .

But I saw something only I could see, because of my astonishing ability to see such things:

Souls were rising, from the earth far below, souls of the dead, of people who had perished, from famine, from war, from the plague, and they floated up, like skydivers in reverse, limbs all akimbo, wheeling and spinning. And the souls of these departed joined hands, clasped ankles and formed a web, a great net of souls, and the souls were three-atom oxygen molecules, of the stuff of ozone, and the outer rim absorbed them, and was repaired.

Nothing's lost forever. In this world, there is a kind of painful progress. Longing for what we've left behind, and dreaming ahead.

At least I think that's so.

EPILOGUE:

Bethesda

February 1990

Prior, Louis, Belize and Hannah sitting on the rim of the Bethesda Fountain in Central Park. It's a bright day, but cold.
Prior is heavily bundled, and he has thick glasses on, and he supports himself with a cane. Hannah is noticeably differ- ent—she looks like a New Yorker, and she is reading the New York Times. *Louis and Belize are arguing. The Bethesda Angel is above them all.*

LOUIS: The Berlin Wall has fallen. The Ceauçescus are out. He's building democratic socialism. The New Interna- tionalism. Gorbachev is the greatest political thinker since Lenin.

BELIZE: I don't think we know enough yet to start canonizing him. The Russians hate his guts.

LOUIS: Yeah but. Remember back four years ago? The whole time we were feeling everything everywhere was stuck, while in Russia! Look! Perestroika! The Thaw! It's the end of the Cold War! The whole world is changing! Overnight!

HANNAH: I wonder what'll happen now in places like Yugoslavia.

PRIOR *(To audience)*: Let's just turn the volume down on this, OK?

They'll be at it for hours. It's not that what they're saying isn't important, it's just . . .

This is my favorite place in New York City. No, in the whole universe. The parts of it I have seen.

On a day like today. A sunny winter's day, warm and cold at once. The sky's a little hazy, so the sunlight has a physical presence, a character. In autumn, those trees across the lake are yellow, and the sun strikes those most brilliantly. Against the blue of the sky, that sad fall blue, those trees are more light than vegetation. They are Yankee trees, New England transplants. They're barren now. It's January 1990. I've been living with AIDS for five years. That's six whole months longer than I lived with Louis.

LOUIS: Whatever comes, what you have to admire in Gorbachev, in the Russians is that they're making a leap into the unknown. You can't wait around for a theory. The sprawl of life, the weird . . .

HANNAH: Interconnectedness . . .

LOUIS: Yes.

BELIZE: Maybe the sheer size of the terrain.

LOUIS: It's all too much to be encompassed by a single theory now.

BELIZE: The world is faster than the mind.

LOUIS: That's what politics is. The world moving ahead. And only in politics does the miraculous occur.

BELIZE: But that's a theory.

HANNAH: You can't live in the world without an idea of the world, but it's living that makes the ideas. You can't wait for a theory, but you have to have a theory.

LOUIS: Go know. As my grandma would say.

PRIOR *(Turning the sound off again)*: This angel. She's my favorite angel.

I like them best when they're statuary. They commemorate death but they suggest a world without dying. They are made of the heaviest things on earth, stone and iron, they weigh tons but they're winged, they are engines and instruments of flight.

This is the angel Bethesda. Louis will tell you her story.

LOUIS: Oh. Um, well, she was this angel, she landed in the Temple square in Jerusalem, in the days of the Second Temple, right in the middle of a working day she descended and just her foot touched earth. And where it did, a fountain shot up from the ground.

When the Romans destroyed the Temple, the fountain of Bethesda ran dry.

PRIOR: And Belize will tell you about the nature of the fountain, before its flowing stopped.

BELIZE: If anyone who was suffering, in the body or the spirit, walked through the waters of the fountain of Bethesda, they would be healed, washed clean of pain.

PRIOR: They know this because I've told them, many times. Hannah here told it to me. She also told me this:

HANNAH: When the Millennium comes . . .

PRIOR: Not the year two thousand, but the Capital M Millennium . . .

HANNAH: Right. The fountain of Bethesda will flow again. And I told him I would personally take him there to bathe. We will all bathe ourselves clean.

LOUIS: Not literally in Jerusalem, I mean we don't want this to have sort of Zionist implications, we . . .

BELIZE: Right on.

LOUIS: But on the other hand we *do* recognize the right of the state of Israel to exist.

BELIZE: But the West Bank should be a homeland for the Palestinians, and the Golan Heights should . . .

LOUIS: Well not *both* the West Bank and the Golan Heights, I mean no one supports Palestinian rights more than I do but . . .

BELIZE *(Overlapping)*: Oh yeah right, Louis, like not even the Palestinians are more devoted than . . .

PRIOR: I'm almost done.

The fountain's not flowing now, they turn it off in the winter, ice in the pipes. But in the summer it's a sight to see. I want to be around to see it. I plan to be. I hope to be.

This disease will be the end of many of us, but not nearly all, and the dead will be commemorated and will struggle on with the living, and we are not going away. We won't die secret deaths anymore. The world only spins forward. We will be citizens. The time has come.

Bye now.

You are fabulous creatures, each and every one.

And I bless you: *More Life*.

The Great Work Begins.

END OF PLAY

Afterword

With a Little Help from My Friends

Angels in America, Parts One and Two, has taken five years to write, and as the work nears completion I find myself thinking a great deal about the people who have left their traces in these texts. The fiction that artistic labor happens in isolation, and that artistic accomplishment is exclusively the provenance of individual talents, is politically charged and, in my case at least, repudiated by the facts.

While the primary labor on *Angels* has been mine, over two dozen people have contributed words, ideas and structures to these plays: actors, directors, audiences, one-night stands, my former lover and many friends. Two in particular, my closest friend, Kimberly T. Flynn (*Perestroika* is dedicated to her), and the man who commissioned *Angels* and helped shape it, Oskar Eustis, have had profound, decisive influences. Had I written these plays without the participation of my collaborators, they would be entirely different—would, in fact, never have come to be.

Americans pay high prices for maintaining the myth of the Individual: We have no system of universal health care, we don't educate our children, we can't pass sane gun control laws,

ANGELS IN AMERICA

we elect presidents like Reagan, we hate and fear inevitable processes like aging and death. Way down close to the bottom of the list of the evils Individualism visits on our culture is the fact that in the modern era it isn't enough to write; you must also be a Writer, and play your part as the protagonist in a cautionary narrative in which you will fail or triumph, be in or out, hot or cold. The rewards can be fantastic; the punishment dismal; it's a zero sum game, and its guarantor of value, its marker is that you pretend you play it solo, preserving the myth that you alone are the wellspring of your creativity.

When I started to write these plays, I wanted to attempt something of ambition and size even if that meant I might be accused of straying too close to ambition's ugly twin, pretentiousness. Given the bloody opulence of this country's great and terrible history, given its newness and its grand improbability, its artists are bound to be tempted towards large gestures and big embraces, a proclivity de Tocqueville deplored as a national artistic trait nearly two hundred years ago. Melville, my favorite American writer, strikes inflated, even hysterical, chords on occasion. It's the sound of the Individual ballooning, overreaching. We are all children of "Song of Myself." And maybe in this spacious, under- and depopulated, as yet only lightly inscribed country, the Individual will finally expand to its unstable, insupportably swollen limits, and pop. (But here I risk pretentiousness, and an excess of optimism to boot—another American trait.)

Anyone interested in exploring alternatives to Individualism and the political economy it serves, Capitalism, has to be willing to ask hard questions about the ego, both as abstraction and as exemplified in oneself.

Bertolt Brecht, while he was still in Weimar-era Berlin and facing the possibility of participating in a socialist revolution, wrote a series of remarkable short plays, his *Lehrstücke*, or learning plays. The principal subject of these plays was the painful dismantling, as a revolutionary necessity, of the individual ego. This dismantling is often figured, in the learning plays, as death.

Brecht, who never tried to hide the dimensions of his own titanic personality, didn't sentimentalize the problems such personalities present, or the process of loss involved in letting go of the richness, and the riches, that accompany successful self-creation.

Brecht simultaneously claimed and mocked the identity he'd won for himself, "a great German writer," raising important questions about the means of literary production, challenging the sacrosanctity of the image of the solitary artist and, at the same time, openly, ardently wanting to be recognized as a genius. That he was a genius is inarguably the case. For a man deeply committed to collectivity as an ideal and an achievable political goal, this blazing singularity was a mixed blessing at best and at worst, an obstacle to a blending of radical theory and practice.

In the lower right-hand corner of the title page of many of Brecht's plays you will find, in tiny print, a list of names under the heading "collaborators." Sometimes these people contributed little, sometimes a great deal. One cannot help feeling that those who bore those minuscule names, who expended the considerable labor the diminutive typography conceals, have gotten a bum deal. Many of these effaced collaborators, Ruth Berlau, Elisabeth Hauptmann, Margarete Steffin, were women. In the question of shared intellectual and artistic labor, gender is always an issue.

On the day last spring when the Tony nominations were being handed out [May 1993], I left the clamorous room at Sardi's thinking gloomily that here was another source of anxiety, another obstacle to getting back to work rewriting *Perestroika*. In the building's lobby I was introduced to the producer Elizabeth I. McCann, who said to me: "I've been worried about how you were handling all this, till I read that you have an Irish woman in your life. Then I knew you were going to be fine." Ms. McCann was referring to Kimberly T. Flynn; an article in the *New Yorker* last year about *Angels in America* described how certain features of our shared experience dealing with her prolonged health crisis, caused by a serious cab accident several years ago, had a major impact on the plays.

Kimberly and I share Louisiana childhoods (she's from New Orleans, I grew up in Lake Charles); different but equally complicated, powerful religious traditions and an ambivalence towards those traditions; Left politics informed by liberation struggles (she as a feminist, I as a gay man), as well as socialist and psychoanalytic theory; and a belief in the effectiveness of activism and the possibility of progress.

From the beginning Kimberly was my teacher. Though largely self-taught, she was more widely read and she helped me understand both Freud and Marx. She introduced me to the writers of the Frankfurt School and their early attempts at synthesizing psychoanalysis and Marxism; and to the German philosopher and critic Walter Benjamin, whose importance for me rests primarily in his introduction into these "scientific" disciplines a Kabbalist-inflected mysticism and a dark, apocalyptic spirituality.

As both writer and talker Kimberly employs a rich variety of rhetorical strategies and effects, even while expressing deep emotion. She identifies this as an Irish trait; it's evident in O'Neill, Yeats, Beckett. This relationship to language, blended with Jewish and gay versions of the same strategies, is evident in my plays, in the ways my characters speak.

More pessimistic than I, Kimberly is much less afraid to look at the ugliness of the world. She tries to protect herself far less than I do, and consequently she sees more. She feels safest, she says, knowing the worst, while most people I know, myself included, would rather be spared and feel safer encircled by a measure of obliviousness. She's capable of pulling things apart, teasing out fundamental concerns from their camouflage; at the same time she uses her analysis, her learning, her emotions, her lived experience, to make imaginative leaps, to see the deeper connections between ideas and historical developments. Through her example I learned to trust that such leaps can be made; I learned to admire them, in literature, in theory, in the utterances people make in newspapers. And certainly it was in part her example that made the labor of synthesizing disparate, seemingly unconnected things become for me the process of writing a play.

Since the accident Kimberly has struggled with her health, and I have struggled to help her, sometimes succeeding, sometimes failing; and it doesn't take much more than a passing familiarity with *Angels* to see how my life and my plays match up. It's always been easier talking about the way in which I used what we've lived through to write *Angels*, even though I sometimes question the morality of the act (while at the same time considering it unavoidable if I was to write at all), than it has been acknowledging the intellectual debt. People seem to be more interested in the story of the accident and its aftermath than in the intellectual genealogy, the emotional life being privileged over the intellectual life in the business of making plays, and the two being regarded, incorrectly, as separable. A great deal of what I understand about health issues comes from what Kimberly has endured and triumphed over, and the ways she's articulated those experiences. But *Angels* is more the result of our intellectual friendship than it is autobiography. Her contribution was as contributor, teacher, editor, adviser, not muse.

Perhaps other playwrights don't have similar relationships or similar debts; perhaps they have. In a wonderful, recently published collection of essays on creative partnerships, entitled *Significant Others*, edited by Isabelle de Courtivron and Whitney Chadwick, the contributors examine both healthy and deeply unhealthy versions of artistic interdependence in such couples as the Delaunays, Kahlo and Rivera, Hammett and Hellman, and Jasper Johns and Robert Rauschenberg— and in doing so strike forcefully at what the editors call "the myth of solitariness."

We have no words for the people to whom we are indebted. I call Oskar Eustis a dramaturg, sometimes a collaborator; but collaborator implies co-authorship and nobody knows what "dramaturg" implies. *Angels*, I wrote in the published version of *Perestroika*, began in a conversation, real and imaginary, with Oskar Eustis. A romantic-ambivalent love for American history and belief in what one of the play's characters calls "the prospect of some sort of radical democracy spreading outward and growing up" are things Oskar and I share, part of the discussions we had for nearly a year before I started writing *Millennium*. Oskar continues to be for me, intellectually and emotionally, what the developmental psychologists call "a secure base of attachment" (a phrase I learned from Kimberly).

The play is indebted, too, to writers I've never met. It's ironical that Harold Bloom, in his introduction to Olivier Revault d'Allonnes' *Musical Variations on Jewish Thought*, provided me with a translation of the Hebrew word for "blessing"—"more life"—which subsequently became key to the heart of *Perestroika*. Harold Bloom is also the author of *The Anxiety of Influence*, his oedipalization of the history of Western literature, which when I first encountered it years ago made me so anxious my analyst suggested I put it away. Recently I had the chance to meet Professor Bloom and, guilty over my appropriation of "more life," I fled from the encounter as one of Freud's *Totem and Taboo* tribesmen might flee from a meeting with that primal father, the one with the big knife. (I cite Bloom as the source of the idea in the published script.)

Guilt plays a part in this confessional account; and I want the people who helped me make this play to be identified, because their labor was consequential. I have been blessed with remarkable comrades and collaborators: Together we organize the world for ourselves, or at least we organize our understanding of it; we reflect it, refract it, criticize it, grieve over its savagery and help each other to discern, amidst the gathering dark, paths of resistance, pockets of peace and places from whence hope may be plausibly expected. Marx was right: The smallest indivisible human unit is two people, not one; one is a fiction. From such nets of souls societies, the social world, human life springs. And also plays.

Tony Kushner
November 15, 1993

ABOUT THE PLAY

Angels in America, Parts One and Two, was commissioned by the Eureka Theatre Company through a special projects grant from the National Endowment for the Arts. The plays were first seen in San Francisco and at the Mark Taper Forum in Los Angeles. Part One: *Millennium Approaches* ran for a year in London at the Royal National Theatre. *Perestroika* opened there, in repertory with a revival of *Millennium*, on November 20, 1993. *Millennium* began its run at the Walter Kerr Theatre on Broadway in May 1993 and was joined by *Perestroika* on November 23, 1993. The Broadway production was followed by an extensive U.S. national tour.

Angels received two Fund for New American Plays/American Express Awards, two Drama Desk Awards for Best Broadway Play of 1993 and 1994, two Outstanding Theatre Awards from the Gay and Lesbian Alliance Against Defamation, two LAMBDA Literary Awards, the 1993 Los Angeles Drama Critics' Award and Tony Awards for Best Play of 1993 and 1994. *Millennium* was awarded the New York, London and San Francisco Drama Critics' Circle Awards for Best Play; the 1993 Outer Critics' Circle Award for Best Broadway Play; the

1991 National Arts Club's Joseph Kesselring Award; the 1991 Will Glickman Award; London's *Evening Standard* Award for Best Play and the 1993 Pulitzer Prize for Drama.

A partial list of additional English-language productions of *Angels* includes the Intiman Theatre Company in Seattle, Washington; the Alliance Theatre Company in Atlanta, Georgia; the American Conservatory Theater in San Francisco, California; the Alley Theatre in Houston, Texas; the Sydney Theatre in Sydney, Australia; the Melbourne Theatre Company in Melbourne, Australia; the Court Theatre in Christchurch, New Zealand; the Adelaide Festival Centre in Adelaide, South Australia; the Theatre Foundation in Auckland, New Zealand; the Circa Theatre in Wellington, New Zealand; the Truk-Pact Repertory of South Africa; and the Abbey Theatre in Dublin, Ireland.

Foreign-language productions have been performed in Buenos Aires, Argentina; Vienna and Lenz, Austria; Brussels, Belgium; Sao Paulo, Brazil; Prague, Czechoslovakia; Copenhagen, Denmark; Aubervilliers (Paris) and Avignon, France; Helsinki, Finland; more than a dozen cities in Germany; Athens, Greece; Rotterdam, Holland; Budapest, Hungary; Reykjavik, Iceland; Tel Aviv, Israel; Rome, Italy; Tokyo, Japan; Oslo, Norway; Manila, Philippines; Gdansk, Poland; Barcelona and Madrid, Spain; Stockholm, Sweden; Zurich, Switzerland; and Montevideo, Uruguay.

In 2003, *Angels in America* was named one of the top five Tony Award–winning plays of all time. It shared this honor with *Death of a Salesman*, *Who's Afraid of Virginia Woolf?*, *The Crucible* and *Long Day's Journey into Night*. It was also chosen by London's Royal National Theatre as one of the Best 100 Plays of the 20th Century.

In 2003, *Angels in America* (Parts One and Two) was made into an epic movie by HBO Films, directed by Mike Nichols.

About the Author

Tony Kushner's plays include *Homebody/Kabul*, *A Bright Room Called Day* and *Slavs!*; as well as adaptations of Corneille's *The Illusion*, Ansky's *The Dybbuk*, Brecht's *The Good Person of Szechuan* and Goethe's *Stella*. Current projects include: *Henry Box Brown or The Mirror of Slavery*; and two musical plays: *St. Cecilia or The Power of Music* and *Caroline or Change*. He is collaborating with Maurice Sendak on an American version of the children's opera, *Brundibar*. Mr. Kushner has been awarded a Pulitzer Prize for Drama, two Tony Awards, the Evening Standard Award, an OBIE, the New York Drama Critics Circle Award, an American Academy of Arts and Letters Award, a Whiting Writers Fellowship, a Lila Wallace/ Reader's Digest Fellowship, and a medal for Cultural Achievement from the National Foundation for Jewish Culture. He grew up in Lake Charles, Louisiana, and he lives in New York.